Date Like a Man

Date Like a Man

To Get the Man You Want and Have Fun Doing It!

Myreah Moore

and Jodie Gould

HarperCollins*Publishers*

HarperCollins books may be purchased for educational, business, or sales promotional use. For information please write: Special Markets Department, HarperCollins Publishers Inc., 10 East 53rd Street, New York, NY 10022.

FIRST EDITION

Designed by Nancy B. Field

Printed on acid-free paper

ISBN 0-06-019498-7

00 01 02 03 04 ❖/HC 10 9 8 7 6 5 4 3 2 1

This book is dedicated with love, respect and gratitude to all the gay men in my life who are no longer on this planet. You helped me learn to treasure myself. Love you madly and miss you very much, my angels!

—MM

To my friends and family (nuclear and extended) for their support and encouragement, and to my husband, Robert Katel, who knew how to date me like a man.

—JG

Contents

Introduction

SO YOU'RE SINGLE. Maybe you've just gone through a divorce or breakup, or maybe you just haven't found the right one yet. Well, congratulations. That's right, congratulations! This can be one of the best times of your life. Being single allows you to discover who you are, what you want for the future, and what you truly need from a man.

Honey, your mother was right when she told you it's a man's world. We've made a lot of progress thanks to our feminist foremothers, but the power scale is still heavily tipped in the man's direction, especially in the dating arena. And all things being unequal, it's time for women to break through the pink ceiling when it comes to romance.

For more than a decade I've been teaching my unique dating philosophy at seminars and one-on-one coaching sessions. I've seen hundreds of women go from scared and lonely to finding their one-and-only. Let's face it, you have to do some training to get yourself into shape for dating. And I don't just mean joining a gym or sweatin' to the oldies. You must train yourself mentally before you start to date.

What Does It Mean to Date Like a Man?

This book will teach you how to stop dating like a woman (for the sole purpose of finding a husband) and start dating like a man (for the purpose of having fun). It will reveal what men already know about dating, and are afraid you'll find out, such as:

- Dating is a numbers game. Men know that the more you date, the more you have to choose from. Women, on the other hand, often end up choosing the first one or the worst one who asks for their hand.
- Dating is a team sport. You don't have to go it alone.
- I will show you how to enlist your friends, neighbors, shopkeepers and colleagues in finding available men.
- Dating means taking risks. Dating means that you might get dumped. So what?! Rejection can open the door to even better dating opportunities.

In addition to having more fun dating, I'll also show you how to narrow your search by separating your "wants" from your "nonnegotiable needs." Ask a man to describe his perfect mate, and he'll probably tell you everything about her right down to the color of her roots.

Ask a woman the same question, and she'll likely talk in generalities. "He's got to be smart," she might say. Does this mean book-smart? Street-smart? I will show you how to ask for, and get, what you want from a man.

As soon as you decide what you want and need, you'll get your wants and needs met. Remember what the Rolling Stones said: "You can't always get what you want, but if you try sometime . . ." You know the rest.

Adjusting Your Dating Attitude

If you think dating is hell, you need to examine what you're doing wrong. Do you feel despondent every time a date turns out to be a dud? Are you constantly checking out your dates for marriage potential? If so, chances are you're taking dating too seriously.

The bottom line is, men understand that dating is fun. If you date like a man, finding a new companion won't be something to fill the time until you happen upon "the one." Women have got to stop seeing marriage as the ultimate goal, the Holy Grail. If marriages were so blissful, why would almost half of them end in divorce? Better to wait, choose well, and do it right the first time.

Look at the bright side! Bad dates make for great conversations with your friends, not to mention free dinners, movies and concert tickets. Guys don't return from a bad date thinking, "What's wrong with me?" They say, "She's the loser."

You've got to get a new dating attitude. If you walk around thinking that you're too fat, too skinny or too old to attract a man, you probably won't. If you believe there are only gay, married or freaky men out there, the men you meet will be gay, married or freaky. Negative thoughts produce negative results.

Once you accept that dating can and should be fun, the days of worrying and searching will be over. You must believe that the person you are looking for can show up at any place at any time. You simply have let go of any negative thoughts that are preventing you from finding your mate.

Finally, *Date Like a Man* will teach you how to be happy without a man, even if you won't be happily single ever after. Honey, I've been there. I'm unmarried, but currently involved with a man whom I adore, and who loves me back. I promise that if you follow my advice and do the exercises in this book, you will feel better about yourself and the men you date. Once you learn to treasure yourself, people will move mountains to be close to you. So get out there and get busy!

PART I

The Warm-Up: Preparing to Date Like a Man

Why Men Are the Master Daters

You've tried *The Rules,* you've tried listening to your married friends, and you've even tried listening to your mother. But you're still eating Chinese takeout with your good *Friends* Monica, Rachel, Ross and Chandler. So how is dating like a man going to change your social life?

Let's start by going back to our cave-dwelling ancestors. According to David Buss, Ph.D., professor of psychology at the University of Texas at Austin, men's reproductive drives cause them to value a woman's youth and physical appearance, and to seek out a variety of sex partners.

Women, in contrast, place a higher premium on a mate's ambition, industriousness and social status to help ensure the survival of the species. Like it or not, these basic biological needs still influence the way men and women date today.

In addition, boys learn from day one how to bond with other children through sports. Sports teach boys how to be competitive and work as a team. Above all, sports encourage them to get out of the house and have fun.

Although many girls growing up today are involved in team sports and have parents who teach them that education, career and self-exploration are also priorities, they are still getting the societal message that love relationships are paramount in their lives.

This fact was confirmed in a recent study conducted at the University of Illinois at Urbana-Champaign. Dr. Karen D. Rudolph, assistant professor of psychology, found that the majority of stress for girls between the ages of eight and eighteen was caused by relationship problems, including fights with their siblings and friends. (Boys were more likely to be stressed about doing poorly in school, getting sick, moving to a new town or getting into trouble.)

Now, I'm not saying that relationships aren't important; men want them, too. But guys also know that having a full life means reaching out beyond your small circle of friends, family and community.

One of the advantages of getting out into the world is discovering what you like and what you don't like. You might also find that nine times out of ten, you're not who you think you are.

Remember the disco queen from the seventies, Donna Summer? She grew up in a large family headed by a preacher father who wanted Donna to stay close to home and sing gospel for his church. But Donna knew in her heart that although she was deeply religious and loved her family, she needed to perform on a larger stage.

She tried the stay-at-home role with her first husband, and felt trapped and miserable. So Donna finally decided to pursue her dream of becoming a pop singer. Sure, there were bad times and bad relationships along the way, but she is now happily remarried with several children and wonderful memories of a career in the spotlight.

Like young birds that need to test their wings, women have got to get out into the world before they start a nest of their own. Remember: Men don't settle down until they find themselves. Women don't settle down until they find a man. Find yourself first, then settle.

Men Know What They Want and Need (And How to Get Those Wants and Needs Met)

I told you in the previous section why it's important to find yourself before you find a man. To do this, you must get out in the world and experience as much as possible. At the same time, however, there are exercises that you must do by yourself and for yourself. I call this doing the inner work.

Doing the inner work is an essential part of dating like a man. Men tend to know exactly they want from a career and from a woman. When I asked a young man named Brian how he saw himself in ten years, he described his house, car, wife and breed of dog in full detail. He had already started saving up to buy that snazzy white Corvette.

Women need to train themselves to focus more clearly on their future goals. Every athlete must train before he or she competes. Doing the inner work is training your mind instead of your body. As your personal dating coach, I will show you why doing the inner work will help you identify what your goals are (your needs) and how you can have those needs met.

First, take out a legal pad, a pencil and a timer or stopwatch. Draw a line down the middle of the paper. On one side write "Wants" and on the other side write "Needs."

Set your timer for ten minutes (I don't want you to agonize over this exercise). Start with the "Wants" list. Write down the characteristics that you want in a mate. If you're done quickly, number them in order of importance, with #1 being the most important.

Be as specific as possible. If you want a man to be tall, do you mean over six feet, or taller than you? Do not censor yourself. Let your heart take control of your mind. Don't worry if your list seems foolish or trivial. If it matters to you, write it down. Remember, if you don't write it down, you won't get what you want. Also, this is *your* wish list, not your mother's or your girlfriend's or your Aunt Julie's.

Here's a sample list that my client Laura made.

Wants

1. Handsome, clean-shaven
2. Over thirty-five
3. Friend first
4. Humorous

5. Educated
6. Politically aware
7. Have a cause in life
8. Christian
9. Kind to animals
10. Kind to kids (will accept my child)
11. Kind to less fortunate people
12. Positive attitude
13. Likes nature walks, shows and aquariums
14. A gentleman
15. Respectful (doesn't curse)
16. Likes to travel
17. Adventurous (likes to try new things, places to eat, life experiences)
18. Laid back, but likes to have fun
19. Can be silly at times and allows me to be silly
20. Honest
21. Someone I can talk to for hours
22. Passionate
23. Likes to move forward, not stagnate
24. Personable, likes to laugh
25. Non-smoker
26. Sophisticated
27. Monogamous
28. High morals
29. Articulate
30. Generous
31. Even-tempered
32. Reliable
33. Clean and neat
34. Family-oriented
35. Can give advice and comfort when I need it

Now, take five minutes to write which of the characteristics on your "Wants" list you *absolutely require* in your mate. These are the things that you are not willing to compromise on, such as intelligence, religion, family-oriented, and so on. Think about your past loves. What did they provide you with? Just as important, which needs didn't they fulfill?

The reason you make this list is to help you determine the type of dating partner you are drawn to. The list also helps you to differentiate between those qualities you'd like to have in a man and those you can't live without.

Now let's examine your lists. Did you find yourself lost after about three minutes, or was ten minutes not enough time? If you couldn't come up with many wants and needs, you need to do more work here until you can come up with at least ten. If you have thirty-five or more wants, like Laura, you should narrow down your list to a top ten.

Here are some other things to consider:

Is your special someone a good listener?
Does he keep his promises?
Is he considerate of others?
Does he have to be a certain coloring or physique?
Does he need to be financially successful?
What are his values and goals?
Does he drink or take drugs?
How important is sexual chemistry?
Is he New Age or Old World?
Is he outgoing or shy?
Is he close to his family and friends?
Are certain hobbies or interests important to you?

The purpose of these lists is to help you find someone who meets your definition of what is right for you. They will also help you to see that no one is absolutely perfect. By prioritizing which qualities are important and which are not, you will discover what you are absolutely unwilling to accept and which less-than-perfect qualities you are willing to overlook.

You will find that there are guys who match every item on the "Wants" list, but didn't do so well on the "Needs" list. Look at your dating history. Were there men in your life who gave you everything you wanted but still weren't enough? Now you know why.

People who have the hardest time doing this exercise are what I call the power brokers. They can pump out a business plan in two minutes flat, but ask them to list their needs in a mate and they're stumped. The power brokers have an easier time describing what they want in an apartment or job than they do in a date or mate.

They've bought into the myth that someday their prince will come, and all they have to do is just wait for him to show up. Lots of people just "show up." But if you're not consciously examining how they fit into your life, you are bound to make mistakes. Would you take the first apartment or house you looked at? Would you hire the first applicant who came along?

What Do Your Wants and Needs Really Mean?

Your wants are your wish list and preferences. They are like the petals on a long-stemmed rose. They are pretty, but they can fall off the stem without killing the entire flower. Your needs are like the strong, healthy stem and roots. They are essential to the survival of the rose. They are the foundation of your relationship.

And, yes, there are thorns in every relationship. They can be painful at times, but they act as self-protective mechanisms. Our thorns come out whenever we feel threatened and defensive. And keep in mind that you can't force a rose to open before it is ready. If you do, it will die.

Your lists are also living organisms. You can edit them

and add to them as you see fit. In the coming months and years, you'll continue to discover characteristics that are important to you in a date or relationship. But you must refer to the lists every time a new man comes into your life. They are your guideline to your dating training program and necessary to keeping your love life on track.

A client named Maggie told me she dated the guy of her dreams when she was in college. They broke up after graduation because she wasn't ready to settle down.

But after years of searching, she was never able to find anyone she liked as much as her college boyfriend. She had done the inner work, so when it came time to write down the qualities that she was looking for in a man, she saw how they matched the qualities that he possessed.

Soon after our session, she ran into her old beau at a funeral. They hit it off immediately, and they are now engaged to be married. Maggie's story proved my theory: You will not be ready until you do the inner work.

Developing Your "Most Wanted" Profile

The third part of your training program involves both action and visualization. You are reading your lists at least once a day. Now that you are aware of your needs, you must create a picture of your soulmate. He may not be America's Most Wanted Man, but he's yours.

To that end, imagine you are talking to a police artist. Describe his hair (blond, brown or jet-black), face (mustache or clean-shaven), and eyes (blue or puppy-dog brown?). Now visualize his physique (chest hair or smooth? brawny or scrawny? tall or small?). Everyone's taste is different.

Meditate on your perfect mate from time to time. Once you have a picture in your mind of your Most Wanted Man, think about the men who are already in your life. Is there anyone who looks like the man in your profile? Remember that your heart's desire can come from anywhere, so do not limit your playing field. Remain open and flexible at all times.

Don't worry if there isn't anyone in your life right now who fits your profile. Continue to think about your Most Wanted Man as if he were already in your life. It will give you an inner strength and confidence, and it will prime you to meet your man when he eventually appears.

Also, keep your fantasy to yourself. Talking about the work you're doing takes energy away from the actual work. Don't share your private miracles with anyone until you have achieved your goals. After that, you can tell everyone how you found your soulmate.

Reflecting on Your Mirror Image

Remember Michael Jackson's song about the man in the mirror? Well, it's time to look at your own reflection, not for wrinkles or blemishes, but for the qualities on your "Wants" and "Needs" lists that you possess.

Surprised? I can't tell you how often women in my seminars put "Must be financially secure" at the top of their "Needs" list. When I ask them if they are financially secure, they stutter, "Ah, no, not really." Well, honey, how do you expect to find a man of wealth if you're flying in coach?

More important, if you don't possess the values that you list as being essential, you will never attract a man with those values. Girlfriend, you are who you attract. In order to attract a man who has the qualities that you want, you *must* have those qualities yourself. Work on attaining the characteristics you're missing, and the man you desire will show up in your life.

If you want a man with money, go out and make some money yourself. If you want a man who is educated but you dropped out of high school, go back to school and get your degree!

If you find yourself dating a man who is dishonest, look at your own life to figure out where you have been dishonest. If the man you're dating is indecisive, ask yourself if you have trouble making decisions as well.

We tend to attract mirror images of ourselves. In this way, dating is part self-exploration. When I asked one of my clients what kind of men she was attracting, she said, "I've been meeting neurotic, insecure men." I said, "Oh, really? And how would you describe yourself?"

"I'm a bit neurotic and insecure myself," she admitted.

"Well, baby, do you think it's a coincidence that you're hooking up with these kinds of men?"

If you're wondering what kind of first impression you make, ask a *male* friend to write down the adjectives that describe you—good and bad. You might be surprised by the answers. I guarantee you that a man will tell you the truth. Women aren't that honest, because they're afraid of hurting people's feelings.

Only when you possess the values and qualities on your lists will you attract a man with similar values and qualities. Once you've done this work, I guarantee that your compatible mate will show up.

But your work isn't over yet (sorry, but these things take time). There is one more checklist you have look at before you zero in on your mate. Here are the four areas that make up a positive relationship:

1. Similar values
2. Mutual respect
3. Physical attraction
4. Common interests

If you do not connect in any of these areas, there's no chance in hell that your relationship will work. And don't think that you will be able to change a man once you're with him. After thirty, unless they are extremely motivated, men do not change who they are.

Many relationships break up because the woman tries to change her man rather than accepting him as he is. This is where you have to refer once again to your "Wants" and "Needs" lists. Let's say you want a man who is "neat and clean," but you don't consider that an essential need in a relationship. You meet a man who has all of the qualities that you need, but also happens to be a slob. He throws his socks and underwear on the floor and piles his dirty dishes in the sink.

While this will no doubt be a source of annoyance for you, it shouldn't be grounds for divorce, because he has other, more important qualities that you need.

Remember:

1. The only person you can ever change is yourself.
2. You must be willing to accept others just the way they are.
3. You must be willing to accept yourself for who you are—or make the appropriate changes.

Stacy, another woman I coached who was a stand-up comedian, went through life with low self-esteem because she had very large breasts. She kept getting involved with men who were only interested in her body. She had a breast reduction, which helped her self-esteem immensely. But what she didn't do was the *inner* work.

She went to California with her new body, ready to start her new life. She called me up recently to tell me she was attracting the same type of men as before. Nothing had changed, and she was still miserable. I said, "Stacy, it doesn't matter how many times you go the gym, or how many colors you dye your hair, or how much surgery you get done. If you don't do the inner work, nothing is going to change."

Until you become the kind of person you're looking for, you will not attract the kind of person you want.

Men Like Themselves

One reason men are the Master Daters is that they believe they can get any woman they want. They can be short, bald, with King Kong fuzz growing on their back, and they still think they can get a Pamela Anderson lookalike. Even if it's just bravado, the simple act of thinking or saying it makes them, on some level, believe it's true.

In contrast, we women think that unless we look like Cindy Crawford, we are forced to settle. In addition, we are often critical of other women who are not perfect. If we find one thing wrong with another woman, if she doesn't have the perfect nose, or she's not at the perfect weight, we say, "She's not so hot!" And we're just as hard, if not harder, on ourselves.

I once had a female co-worker who was critical of everyone, calling one woman we worked with "a fat pig." I finally asked her why she said such harsh things. She said, "Because it's true. Besides, I'm a fat pig, too."

I told her that she might be overweight, but she wasn't a pig. By lashing out at other people, she was really lashing out at herself. We all have flaws, inside and out. People who are hypercritical of others are often basically unhappy with themselves.

Men give each other more encouragement and support. Their pal might weigh 250 pounds or be coyote ugly, and their buddies will tell him he's a prize (whether they believe it or not). "She wants you, man," they'll egg each other on with the slap of a palm. "Just go for it!"

I'll grant you that this is no easy feat for women, but we must *feel* good about ourselves exactly the way we are. We may want to improve ourselves, but we must believe that there is nothing wrong with the *essential* person we are inside and out.

Men support each other because they understand that they are only as strong as their weakest link. When the ugly guy gets the pretty girl, it benefits all of mankind. It shows them that they, too, can be less than perfect and get the girl. As women, we should stop being so critical of each other and adopt a little more team spirit.

Borrowing once again from the guys' dating handbook, the next time you're on the beach, observe the way men behave. Guys tend to strut around unselfconsciously whether they're fresh-from-the-gym buff or in their pot-bellied, hair-receding glory. They look in the mirror and say, "Not bad." I don't have to tell you what happens when women look at themselves in the mirror.

Loving yourself means accepting your imperfections and finding someone who will love and accept them, too. It all has to do with the way you perceive yourself. If you really believe you're special, inside and out, you will attract a man who is special. I've met many average-looking women who have men around them all the time. They're desirable because of who they think they are and what they think they can offer.

Before you go on a date, tell yourself you are every man's dream. A woman who has confidence in her walk and talk will turn heads, even if she's not a beauty.

If you happen to be pretty, be proud of your looks. If you're smart, use your brains, because that's your power source. If you're funny, be the wittiest woman in the room. Find your strength, build on that, and know that's why a man will want to be with you.

Confidence is contagious. The more powerful and confident you feel, the more powerful and confident men you will attract. Mae West (the "come up and see me sometime" actress from the thirties) was not exactly skinny, but she was a sensual woman who had men clamoring to be with her. Every fiber of her ample being said, "I'm special, so you better keep your eyes on the prize."

So how do you learn to like your imperfect self more when all you see on TV and in magazines are skinny, beautiful babes? Here's how: Stop reading the fashion magazines and watching the commercials that feature perfect-looking creatures. Use that mute button on the remote control and look away when the offending ad comes on the air. Bring a book to the hairstylist and doctor's office rather than pore through the magazines. Or read *Time or Newsweek* instead of *Vogue* or *Harper's Bazaar*.

When I was in my early twenties, I spent $25 a week on fashion magazines. I felt terrible about the way I looked. As soon as I stopped buying those magazines and started seeing the real me instead of the woman I thought I *should* be, I stopped hating myself.

Our minds are like computers. If you program yourself to think, "I'm not good enough," that's what you'll boot up every time you meet someone new. If you program the message to say, "I'm great just the way I am," it will show on your face and body and in the way you carry yourself.

Now, we all get a buzz from seeing pretty women in nice clothes, so this fashion fast doesn't have to last forever. You can resume your normal eye-candy grazing as soon as you feel better about yourself. But if seeing emaciated models makes you want to pop some Ex-Lax after eating—throw the damn magazines away!

If you find yourself staring at your face or body for thirty minutes each day, give yourself twenty-five minutes of hate and then stop. Keep your eye on the clock and force yourself to walk away after twenty-five minutes. The next time you feel the urge to do this, reduce the time to twenty.

Then fifteen, ten, five, and so on, until you just glance at yourself or you stop obsessing altogether.

Men don't spend hours contemplating the circumference of their hips and thighs. Why should we? Look at Howard Stern. He's gangly, he has a big nose, and he is, admittedly, underendowed. How does he deal with his flaws? He jokes about them. He even *brags* about them. But the message he conveys to every model or actress who walks into his studio is, "I'm one sexy dude." Love him or hate him, women can take a lesson from Stern.

Men understand that they are unique individuals—and you are, too! Don't close yourself off just because you don't live up to some advertised ideal. Real men want real women.

Take it from me. Once upon a time I weighed 285 pounds. Much of that weight is now just a memory, but I'll never forget how much I hated myself back then. Then I met my friend Veronica, who weighed just as much. While I was hanging around the house feeling sorry for myself, she always had two or three guys showering her with attention.

What did she have that I didn't? You guessed it: a positive self-image. She never saw herself as fat. She never made excuses for the dress size she wore. She would say, "Honey, there's just more of me to love."

Veronica never wore big, baggy camouflage clothes. "If they want me," she said, "they'll want my body, too—just as it is." She loved doing a striptease for her boyfriends with the lights *on*. Veronica was sexy in her own way, and men adored her.

Today, Veronica is married to a successful man who loves her and takes her all around the world. And believe me, she still thinks of herself as quite a catch (and so does her husband).

The lesson I learned from Veronica is that to find the men of our dreams, we must think of ourselves as date magnets. A woman who knows she is sexy doesn't waste her time with men who aren't interested in her. I used to go to parties and have one or two men asking for my phone number, while twenty-five others wouldn't give me a second glance. So what? I always say, If a guy doesn't want to be with me because I'm not 105 pounds, I don't want to be with him either!

Men Don't Think of Themselves As Victims

Many women go through life thinking of themselves as victims. And while it's tragic to think how many of us were reared in dysfunctional households or worse, have been harassed, raped or victims of incest, there comes a time when we must take responsibility for our lives and move on.

Girlfriend, don't get stuck in a pit of self-pity by saying, "He did this to me" and "She did that to me." Get professional help, own the problem and let it go. If you find yourself feeling like a victim, you are definitely not ready to date. You are only setting yourself up for being a victim once again. Victims often send out emotional flares that say, "This is the way I'm used to being treated." They might even take out their anger on their mates and children.

You need to go back and do more of the inner work (see page 4). Only when you've taken care of yourself can you begin to take care of others.

Men Are Independent

Men want women who are happy, healthy and full of energy, not someone who will drag them down with despair and clinging dependence. No man sees a woman going through a difficult time and says, "I wish I could take care of her." This happens only in the movies. Men are independent, and they want women who can take care of themselves.

A couple should complement each other by being two equal halves of a whole. If you split a ripe, juicy apple down the middle, you will have two delicious pieces of fruit. If part of the apple is rotting, you cut off the bad piece and throw it away so it doesn't ruin the rest of the fruit. That's how men feel when their girlfriends or wives have become a burden to them: They want to cut them out of their lives.

The new millennium woman may want to have a man in her life, but she doesn't *need* a man to take care of her or make decisions for her. Honey, you want sugar, not a sugar daddy. Men respect women who value their independence. You may not have to make as much money as he does (women still don't meet men dollar for dollar in this economy), but you should be willing to do your fair share.

An Independent Woman . . .

Knows how to change a flat tire.
Doesn't mind eating or traveling alone.
Pays her own rent or mortgage.
Dates a man even though her friends may not like him.
Enjoys a regular girls' night out.
Always has some money stashed away for emergencies.
Has an area of expertise.
Doesn't put her social life on hold because she's waiting for her prince to come.

And you should never expect a man to come to your emotional rescue. This is what therapists are for. An emotionally dependent woman is just as much of a burden as a financially dependent one. Get help and get healthy *before* you start dating, not afterward.

Men Know That Money Is Sexy

Unless they are independently wealthy, men know that they have to work in order to be successful. As long as this is true, a woman will never be on an equal footing with a man unless she has money of her own.

In the past, women weren't allowed into the business world; they were forced to acquire money by marrying well. Darlin', back then, a woman would marry the Hunchback of Notre Dame if she thought he owned the cathedral. And who can blame our foresisters? Marriage and inheritance were the only ways a woman could get financial security.

Well, welcome to the twenty-first century. We still may not earn as much as men do, but there's no reason on earth why we should depend on men for our livelihood.

Going after a man because he's rich is a personal decision; I won't dissuade you if that's what you really want. Remember that blond bimbette, Anna Nicole Smith, from dirt-poor Texas, who married the ninety-nine-year-old tycoon? He got to bury his head in her voluminous breasts, while she got his money after he was buried. If that's what you want, fine.

But I believe it's a hell of a lot better to make the money yourself. You won't have to haggle with lawyers, ex-wives and snubbed relatives. Besides, if you happen to meet an equally wealthy guy (and you probably will, because you'll be traveling in those circles), you'll be twice as rich!

Although men don't generally woo women for their money, younger men prefer being with women who work.

There is a mutual respect that comes from both of you being out in the trenches, dealing with bosses, co-workers, promotions, demotions and so on. You have more in common, and there's a lot more to talk about when you both get home! The question of whether or not to stay at home can be addressed when children come into the picture.

And no matter how important raising a family is, stay-at-home moms do not get the respect they deserve from men. You never hear about "breeding power" unless you're talking about racehorses, but you do hear about "earning power." This goes under the heading of it ain't fair, but that's the way it is.

Men Know That Power Is Sexy

Women have always been attracted to powerful men. So if power turns you on, don't apply for a job as a nurse, corporate secretary or White House intern. That's thinking small. Get an M.D., MBA or law degree and get yourself some influence!

But you must start by developing your T&A (talents and assets). What are your accomplishments? Can you landscape a garden like that diva of domesticity Martha Stewart? Can you join the Cabinet, or are you able to make your own? Can you teach a classroom of thirty children how to read? Now that's power, baby.

I've asked every woman I've coached who has told me she wanted a powerful man, "Are *you* powerful?" Become the person you're looking for. You are who you attract. The days of the woman behind the man are over. You are the woman *beside* the man, never behind.

Nowadays, powerful men are looking for women who have their own full lives (remember what I said about getting out into the world?). They're (rightfully) suspicious of women who are interested only in their wallets. You can't do anything for them that they can't do for themselves. Dazzle him with your own power.

Power isn't just having influence over companies and countries. Power is the ability to ask for what you want. Power is making a request and having the courage to accept that the other person might say no. Power is understanding that being turned down has nothing whatsoever to do with your real value as a person.

Power is being comfortable with who you are, and knowing that people will want to spend time with you. Power is knowing that if someone you're interested in doesn't ask you out, it's his loss.

I'm coaching a woman now who is dating a major celebrity. She's a smart, beautiful graduate student who is panicking because this man, who can get any woman he sets his sights on, has expressed interest in her. She asked for my help in trying to "bag" him.

First of all, I told her that you don't ever want to "catch" a man; you want him to catch you! Men don't want to feel like prey. They are historically the hunters and biologically the pursuers, and they like it this way.

But my client's biggest mistake is seeing him as a celebrity and not as a regular guy. I told her to stop going after him because he has fame and fortune, and start looking at him as if he's some poor slob that nobody knows.

The truth is, powerful men are so used to people kissing their butts that they're often attracted to women who say, "Baby, you are not all that." Only then will he see her as someone who is interested in the person he really is, rather than simply the trappings of success.

Dating Training Films

Every day women are bombarded with messages about love, dating, relationships and marriage. We get it from the ads we see, the magazines we read and the sitcoms and soaps we watch.

But nothing is quite as powerful as the movies, where we get two or more full hours of a mind-absorbing, heartrending, tear-jerking drama or romantic comedy that stays with us long after the last kernel of popcorn has been consumed.

Unless we analyze them for the lessons they convey, we are in danger of blurring the lines between fact and fiction. I encourage you gather 'round your girlfriends, rent the following dating training films, and look for their not-so-hidden messages.

Gone With the Wind **(1939), Victor Fleming, director**

No other film has been more imprinted into the female psyche than this one. Most women can lip-synch every word of the dialogue. We like it because the heroine, although the epitome of Old World femininity, is no pushover. She is smart, strong-willed and resourceful.

But the real hook comes from the unrequited love she has for Ashley (can this name ever be uttered without being breathless?) and the macho man who truly does give a damn, Rhett.

Rhett's appeal comes from his attempt to tame the shrewish Scarlett by deciding that she is a woman who "should be kissed, and kissed often, by someone who knows how." Every woman secretly wants to be rescued by a man like Rhett, especially if he's a good kisser.

The problem is, Rhett is an Alpha Man. He's a gambler and a drunk who makes money while the country is at war. He enjoys the company of prostitutes (Belle Watling) who visit him while he's in jail.

He is also an opportunist; he rejects his fellow Confederates when he thinks the North is going to win, only to return to his native Dixieland later (leaving Scarlett and the ailing Melanie to make their way through the burning city of Atlanta).

Men Know They Can Be Sexy At Any Age

While it's true that our culture cherishes its youth, I believe women in their forties and fifties can have even more fun dating than women in their twenties. Here's why: *Mature women are old enough to know what they want.*

Dating after a divorce or breakup can be scary for many women because they are used to someone telling them what they can or cannot do. Not anymore! Being single again means that the only one you have to answer to is yourself.

If you've been married for decades and you're suddenly single, you have an opportunity to rediscover your own power and brilliance. Baby, you have so much more to be grateful for and so much more to offer a man; a twenty-year-old doesn't know what she has to offer yet.

Dating post-forty is about blowing the dust off your dreary social life and enjoying your newfound freedom. It's about not putting things off until tomorrow; it's about following your heart's desire, wherever that may lead.

Sure, men want to sleep with nubile young women, but they also want someone who is fun to be with after they pull their socks on and get out of bed. If you know how to have fun, you will attract men at any age. The biggest complaint couples have about being married is that they've stopped having fun together. Being newly single is the time to recapture the feeling of excitement you get kissing someone for the first time. (See "How to Have Sex Like a Man" on p. 161.)

Plus, as women, we don't reach our sexual prime until we're in our thirties. We have a better sense of our bodies and what we can do with them! A woman doesn't really come into her full power until she's in midlife. Only then do you have the courage to do things that you would never have done before. Who's going to tell you not to? You're a grown-up. You can live until you're one hundred, so there are lots of great times ahead of you.

Don't worry about not having perky breasts or a washboard stomach. Those things have nothing to do with what you have to contribute to the world. Besides, if you really want breasts that stand up and salute, you can buy them. Plastic surgery isn't just for movie stars anymore. Or you can exercise and maintain a healthful diet to look younger and feel more vibrant.

But keep in mind that the women we truly admire are not the most beautiful women in the world. They are the women who are comfortable with themselves and their role in life. Women who possess this knowledge can take your breath away. Eleanor Roosevelt, Amelia Earhart, Betty Ford, Helen Gurley Brown, Gloria Steinem, Rosa Parks, and Oprah Winfrey are all examples of women we admire for their authenticity, power and integrity. Get the outer work done, if you think you *really* need it, but not until you've done your inner work.

Another great thing about being older is having the courage to say no. I'm not talking about sex and drugs here, I'm talking about not wasting time doing things out of obligation or fear of what someone else will think about you. We no longer have to do what our parents tell us, or what our friends think is the cool thing to do. We know how to run our life and business on our own terms. And if that ain't sexy, I don't know what is!

Men Understand the "Vision Thing"

Even in this oh-so-evolved twenty-first century, women still limit themselves by thinking small. The things that your parents or girlfriends might want out of life are not necessarily what will make you happy. Your friend might dream about a family and a house in the suburbs, while your fantasy might involve being a singer, doctor, writer or ambassador. The only way you'll really know for sure is to surround yourself with people who symbolize what you want be.

Men are taught in the playpen to dream BIG. They understand what President George Bush called the "vision thing." Honey, you've got to dream just as BIG, even if it feels ridiculous at first, because it will open your world to enormous possibilities. I promise.

An example of thinking big when you're dating is saying, "I want to be a couple like John and Katherine MacArthur, the philanthropists who give out the 'genius awards.' I want to find someone with whom I can make a contribution to the world." That's a lot bigger goal than, "I want to find a husband."

Or maybe your dream is to raise a family of sane, happy and healthy children who will grow up to do good things for other people. That vision will surely inform the kind of man you want to be with—and that's a lot bigger than wanting someone to care for you in your old age. Having a vision for your future is much larger than having a goal.

I have a friend named Elizabeth who was once a limited thinker. She's a bright, attractive actress in her early forties. As successful as she is in her career, she doesn't feel valuable when she doesn't have a man in her life. She runs around in a panic with inappropriate, subpar men because "they're better than nothing" and that's all she thinks she deserves.

Because she's coming from a limited place ("I'll never find anyone good enough to marry"), she's attracting men who are equally limited. She's willing to settle for less in the hope that she can mold her men into something that they're not. Baby, if you don't like your man *before* you get married, you're going to want to see him dead or divorced before too long.

I told Elizabeth that she had to stop looking at herself as someone who needed to compromise and see herself as the treasure that she is. Once we rid of ourselves of limited thinking, we can fill that empty place with limitless possibilities.

Remember that great sports fable *Field of Dreams*? (If you don't, you should read the book or see the movie starring Kevin Costner.) The moral of the story is, "If you build it, they will come." In other words, if you dream big, there will be at least nine men playing catch in your backyard.

Having a vision for the future will not only help you when you're dating, it will help you to develop your life goals. By creating a vision that is so compelling, you will want to take the first steps toward achieving your goals immediately, be it a husband, a career or a creative pursuit.

PART II

Master Daters are players, and that's exactly what you will become once you understand some basic truths about the way men think and date.

Becoming a Master Dater means being at the top of your game. This includes having excellent form, timing and technique; it's knowing when to make your move, and when to sit it out. Here are some tips to help guide you through the process of becoming a player.

Men Know Dating Is a Numbers Game

Men like numbers. That's why so many of them are good at math. It's also the reason I developed my Pair and a Spare philosophy (dating at least three men at once). This is the number that has worked for me, and for hundreds of my clients and workshop attendees. Perhaps two will be enough for you. If you're truly energetic, maybe you'll want to date four or five. There's no such thing as having too many men in your life!

For starters, I believe that every woman should date a minimum of one hundred men before she chooses a mate. When you think about the fact that we start dating as teenagers, that's really not as many dates as it sounds. Now remember, I said, "date," not "sleep with."

In fact, when it comes to sex with the man you are *really* serious about, I believe you should wait at least four months. If you think you can't do it, I'll give you some tips later on for getting through it (and how to help prove to him that you're worth waiting for). What are a few months if you've got a lifetime to be together?

If you're not in a committed relationship right now, you need to get out there and circulate. In real estate it's location, location, location. Well, when it comes to dating, it's circulation.

You must see and, more important, *be seen by* as many men as possible. Guys don't sit by the phone or computer waiting for someone to call or e-mail. Darlin', you're a girl on the go with lots of options. If you're out on the town with Mike and not sitting at home pining for Phil, you can be cool instead of overeager when Phil finally calls.

You may think this is unnecessary game playing, but let's be real. Dating is a sport, and men love sports. I hate it when women come to my classes and say, "I don't want to play games." Well, honey, then you don't want to date.

One of my clients, a young woman named Christine, was an accountant at a New York radio station. She was attracted to a guy in sales named Mark. They used to chat around the coffeemaker, where he would smile and flirt with her and she'd smile and flirt back. This went on for months, and he never asked her out for a date.

I told Christine to make sure that Mark saw her going out with other men. She invited a few of her male friends to the office and introduced them to her boss and colleagues. The gossip mill started buzzing. It was only after Mark saw Christine with other men, whom he believed to be her suitors, that he asked her out.

When twenty-three-year-old Caroline came to see me, she was having trouble with her boyfriend, Jason. They had been dating for several months, and one night, over a romantic dinner, he leaned over and told her she was "special." Two days later, he went off on a vacation with his pals without as much as a "See you later."

The next time he and Caroline went out, he told her he wanted her to meet his mother. The following day he cancelled their Friday night movie date because "something had come up" at work. Talk about mixed signals.

Caroline was ready to call it quits. But before she did that,

I told her to try an experiment: She had to make herself completely unavailable to him. That weekend, she went out with a friend who was visiting from out of town. When she came back late that evening, there were fifteen messages on her answering machine. "It's noon, where are you?" "It's eight o'clock. Why haven't you called me back?" Jason was ballistic.

When she finally called him, she told him she was "out with a friend." Period. She didn't give him any more information. Given his recent behavior, it was none of his business what she was doing.

A week later, he presented her with two tickets to St. Thomas for their first trip together. It's been paradise ever since. It's not that Caroline tricked Jason into a commitment (trickery never lasts in the long run), she simply helped him to focus more clearly on what he wanted—her! Caroline expedited Jason's commitment to her by following my three dating steps:

> **Step #1. Date Him.** Do you like the guy? Do you think that you have a lot in common? Go out with him two or three times to see if you click. Let him woo *you*.
> **Step #2: Disappear.** Make yourself totally unavailable. He'll call you and get your answering machine. If he drops by your house, your blinds will be drawn. Keep him in a state of deprivation for about a week.
> **Step #3: Reestablish Contact.** After a week's hiatus, pick up the phone and pop back into his life. Don't apologize for your absence or make excuses. Just tell him you've been very busy. Then ask him, "What's new with you?"

I learned these steps from (who else?) men. Have you ever been one of many entries in a man's little black PowerBook? Well, let me empower *you*. While you're driving the man you're truly interested in crazy wondering what you're doing when you're not with him, you'll be out having fun. I know it sounds harsh, but that's what the game is all about. And you've got to be in it to win it!

Juggling a Pair and a Spare requires a plan and a schedule. Keep a datebook. Wednesdays are for Tom. Fridays are for Rick. And it shouldn't be a secret that you're dating other men. Remember, before you get serious, before there is any commitment, you are both free to date whomever you choose, whenever you choose. We women tend to forget that and focus on one guy at a time.

Once you start your Pair and a Spare program, you will find yourself with very little free time—you're too busy dating! Never make yourself available to the men you're dating whenever they call.

This happened to my client Jenny. When I asked her how her Pair and a Spare dating program was going, she said she enjoyed dating several men at once, but her girlfriends disapproved. They told her she was acting like a slut for dating more than one man at a time. They asked her, "Who do you think you are, Cindy Crawford?"

I asked a male client named Ben the same question. He told me everything was going great, and that his friends high-five him every time he tells them about his dates.

Why the discrepancy? Because Jenny's friends, who are also single, are buying into the double standard. It's okay for men to date many women, but it's not okay for women to do the same. He's a player, she's a slut.

It's also possible that they're jealous of the fact that Jenny's having fun and they're not. She's no longer in what I call the Misery Club, and misery, as we all know, loves company. So they choose to dismiss her as promiscuous, rather than see her as victorious, which is what she is.

Surround yourself with positive-thinking friends. If your pals ask you how you can justify juggling so many men at once, tell them, "I'm having a wonderful time, and I'm not hurting anyone. I hope you can happy for me."

You can also tell them, "I'm not sleeping with these men, I'm dating them. They're my friends, not my lovers." The best way to handle questions like, "Is he a boyfriend, or what?" is to say, "He's my sweetie." It's vague enough to imply intimacy without a sexual relationship. Referring to all your dates as your sweeties is the truth, as all the men you know should bring some sweetness into your life.

You can also invite the naysayers to take a break from the Misery Club and join you on your dating crusade. Offer to set them up with one of the men you've dated in past who wasn't quite right for you, but might make a good match for them. See how quickly they change their tune after that!

Even with the Pair and a Spare method, there is no reason to go out every night of the week. Everyone needs time to reflect and be alone. In the beginning, never see a date more than once a week. If you see a man every night, you will overwhelm him, and that relationship will be over as quickly as it got started. Men value what they can't easily get.

By prolonging the anticipation and maintaining a little mystery about yourself, I guarantee that you will make him want you even more.

Men will complain about this kind of gamesmanship, but they'll also admit that it works. Don't cop an attitude when he calls. Be pleasant, friendly and interested. It doesn't matter what you're doing, as long as you're busy. If he wants to see you on Friday and Saturday night, tell him you'd love to see him, but the weekend is not good. How about Thursday?

All men know that it's human nature not to value what is easy to come by. If someone wants to sell you a car for $100, how valuable do you think that jalopy is? But a brand-new Mercedes, while costing more, is far more desirable. If you put your money away every month to finance that beautiful, shiny Mercedes, it will last longer and you will appreciate it more. Which would you rather be: a Mercedes or a used car?

Remember, if the relationship doesn't work out, don't despair. Go back to your dating pool and check his number. Was he number fifteen, twenty-five or forty-five? How many more do you have left before you've dated a hundred men? Then tell yourself, "Okay, I have seventy-five men to go before I find the right one for me." Girl, you've got time. Don't rush into any relationship that doesn't fit your wants and needs criteria.

Any training, whether it's sports or dating, involves practice. The more you do it, the better you'll get at it. Once you've dated five hundred men, you know exactly what you want. You'll also give yourself much-needed time to learn who you are.

Give yourself the time to learn. Women often feel that if they don't find the right one right away, something's wrong. The truth is, you've got to learn before you earn.

Men Believe There Are Too Many Women, There Is Too Little Time

Remember when your grandmother told you there's a lid for every pot? She was right. But despite Grandma's wisdom, many women don't believe this to be true. We continue to believe in a man shortage.

"They're all married, they're all gay, they're all dogs," and so on. This is crazy, negative thinking. And when we finally meet a man who fulfills a few of our needs, we grab him because "he's better than most," or because "at least I'm not sitting at home on a Saturday night." Well, honey, that's not good enough.

Men, on the other hand, operate as if there is an abundance of women. The truth is, darlin', there are more than enough good men in the world. If you don't believe it, go into an online chat room using a female-sounding screen name and see how many men try to strike up a conversation with you. Not all of them will be perfect for you, but at least you'll see that they're out there!

Those of you who think there aren't enough good men out there might simply be too shy to talk to unfamiliar men. Shyness creates real feelings of anxiety, depression and loneliness. It encourages you to think too much about your shortcomings and to become overly preoccupied with your reactions to things and other people. Your shyness can also affect the way others perceive you. (Shy people are often mistaken for being stuck-up or arrogant.)

Listen up, my shy and insecure sisters. I'm not going to tell you not to think the way you do about yourself, because those feelings are real, even if they aren't true. But I am going to tell you how *men* think. And since men think in sports terms, here's the tip: If you're going to play the game, you've got to step up to the plate and swing the bat. You might get hit by the ball, and you might even get injured. Maybe you'll strike out. Even Mark McGwire, the all-time home run hitter, strikes out once in a while.

Girlfriend, you've got to do whatever it takes to start getting out and meeting people. Start by saying hello to one person a day. Once you feel comfortable with that, make it two. Then three, four and on and on.

The next step is making small talk. I don't care if it's as boring as a comment about the weather. Practice starting a conversation. The more you do it, the more comfortable you'll feel. I promise.

Whatever you do, you've got to come out of hiding and declare your availability. It doesn't matter how you fill up your dance card, as long as you take some action. If you're too shy to take out a personal ad, have a friend or family member fix you up with someone who they think is a good match.

Men run in packs, so if you have a nice male friend, workmate or neighbor, chances are he has other nice male friends. Network! Tell your neighbors. Tell the postman. Get the word out.

What you think is what you create. Your words and thoughts are powerful. If you keep to yourself, if you are afraid to show the world who you are, the world won't notice. Try retraining yourself by doing this exercise for one month: Every day start thinking, writing, saying and singing:

"I feel like a kid in a candy shop."
"It's raining men, hallelujah!"
"So many men, so little time."

It may sound silly to you at first, but it works. If it makes you giggle, fine. One more reason to let a nice man catch you in a smile. Repeat this mantra for a while, or make up one of your own with a similar message, and see who shows up. Unless you're living in a nunnery (in which case, you shouldn't be reading this book!), there will be men all around you.

At the same time, make a list of all the men you come into contact with in a given week. Include everyone from your workmates, classmates and gym mates to the man who cuts your meat at the butcher shop. (If you're a vegetarian, the bearded guy who pours your soybeans.)

Add the men you don't see every day, but know through a friend of a friend of a friend. Your roommate's brother, your girlfriend's brother's friends, your cousin's college buddy, your married friend's brother's friend. The guy who walks your dog, the guy whose dog you walk. Open yourself up to all possibilities.

Try not to limit yourself by thinking someone is beneath or above your status. That guy behind the counter at Starbucks might be the next Steven Spielberg or working his way through law school. Or that high-powered attorney who helped negotiate the closing of your house or apartment might be longing to go out with someone who isn't a lawyer.

Don't worry about what someone's occupation is for now. You're not looking for a husband yet. You're looking for dates. Stop worrying that he's too short, poor, shy, bold, whatever. Men beget men. Don't think about the ultimate goal (especially if your goal is to get married)—think about having fun!

Men Don't Worry About Potential

Some men will date any woman who says yes. Most women will only date men who have potential (i.e., marriage possibilities). That kind of thinking gets us into trouble, because once we think we have a guy with potential, we feel we have to develop him. As a result, we get fixated on one single guy.

The first thing you've got to do is let go of the concept of potential. Why would you want someone you need to fix? Have you ever known a man to say about a woman he's dating, "She's nice, but I'm going to try to help her come out of her shell"?

Men don't try to change the women they're dating because they're too busy doing other things. If they want to be with a woman, they'll be with her. If she's high-maintenance, he'll either dump her or accept her for who she is.

Women shouldn't try to be relationship mechanics. It's like buying a bad car. Why waste your money trying to fix a lemon? Just trade it in for a better one. Men are not going to change. If you're spending more time and energy trying to change a man than having fun with him, you don't want to be with him.

Stop looking for a husband and start looking for a companion. Use your female relationships as models. Are they strong and secure? Do you accept that your friends have certain problems and idiosyncrasies? Do you spend all your time trying to change them? My guess is, probably not.

Your goal isn't to find a friend who will be with you for the rest of your life. If that happens, it's great; if the friendship breaks up or fades away with time, while there is often sadness, you generally feel that you've enjoyed their company for however long it lasted. Unless something ugly has occurred, you don't feel wounded. It's a much saner way to handle relationships, don't you think?

When women date men they ask themselves, "Is this the man I want to be with forever?" A woman worries about the future until she finds a husband. A man doesn't start worrying about the future until he finds a wife. Don't fast-forward your relationship! Take the time to enjoy each other. You may be together for three months or three years. Stay in the present until you're sure that there will be a future.

I know it's hard, but you've got to relax and maintain a playful spirit. If your date ends up as your friend, that's great. If not, that's okay, too.

Men Don't Talk About Relationships

In addition to wanting to be in a relationship, women like *talking* about being in a relationship. This is fine if you're with your girlfriends who are equally obsessed, but this constant temperature-taking sends men into nervous spasms.

You can break yourself of this bad habit by understanding the following:

- Until you've been with a guy for at least four months, you are not yet in a relationship. You are dating!

- Until you fall in love with a guy and he falls in love with you, you do not have a relationship.
- Until you've been dating him for nearly a year, you are not in love. You can be in lust. You can be infatuated. You can be strongly in like. But love takes time. Love is the diploma at the end of the course. Love is the gold medal you get after months of training.

By not constantly talking about your relationship, you will have much more time to enjoy the experience of being together.

Men Don't Overanalyze

This is a basic difference between the genders. Women like to analyze everything. We'll ask our dates, "What did you mean by that?" or "How did it make you feel when your ex-girlfriend dumped you for your best friend?"

The fact is, men don't want to discuss their past relationships or their relationship with their mothers while they're out on a date. They want to have fun. You are not his therapist! The only thing a man wants to do on a couch is roll around with you.

Resist the temptation to analyze his every sentence, gesture or expression. If you're currently in therapy, don't tell him about your last session or how you discovered that you need a father figure in your life, especially if you've figured out that he fulfills that role for you. Keep your revelations to yourself, and keep the conversation light and breezy, especially when you are first dating.

The same goes for dream interpretation. Dreams are interesting to the person who's had them. Long stories with jump cuts from scene to surreal scene can be tedious, unless, of course, you're being paid $100 an hour to listen to them. Don't bore your date with your dreamscapes just because you want to divulge your innermost thoughts or test certain scenarios out on him, such as, "I had this dream we got married!"

If you happen to belong to some self-help group like Mindspring, keep that to yourself as well, at least for the first few months. Never, ever try to recruit your date. Consider those things hobbies, not religions. Likewise, if you're a born-again Christian or Orthodox Jew, you will probably need to stay within the flock when dating. Even when you're open to interfaith relationships, resist the temptation to convert your date.

Don't even tell him you're reading this book. Once you've reached your goal, you can talk about how you succeeded. It's like dieting. Once you've lost the weight, you can tell people how you did it. Sharing the process while it's happening, however, is more like watching the grass grow.

Men Don't Feel Comfortable in Homes That Are Too Feminine

Most men feel uncomfortable in houses or apartments that are too frilly. If you plan to invite your dates over to your place for dinner or a video, go easy on the lace, pink and Victoriana. Don't put cozies on your bathroom tissue box. You're not his grandmother.

When I find too many cute stuffed animals in a female client's apartment, I tell her to keep her favorite one and give the others to some needy child or charity.

The same goes for those damned Beanie Babies. Whatever you do, don't display your dolls on the bed like it's some freaky stuffed animal farm. Having too many dolls or teddy bears sends the message to a man that you're not ready to have a grown-up relationship. It's one thing for him to have to compete with other suitors for your affections, and it's another for him to have to compete with inanimate objects.

Antiques are beautiful, but there should be somewhere in your house or apartment where you and your date can kick back, put your feet up, eat and feel relaxed. If a man is too worried about water rings or breakage, he's not going to be able to concentrate on you.

I have an aunt who has stacks of china and linens that she never uses because she's waiting for the right occasion. So far that occasion has yet to come. I asked her one day, "Aunt Margaret, who are you waiting for, the Queen of England? Why don't you use that stuff?"

You don't have to leave the good china and linens in the closet gathering dust. Take out the good stuff when you're having your girlfriends over, throwing an office party, or preparing a romantic candlelight dinner for your beau.

Otherwise, when entertaining men, stick with sturdy everyday dishes and paper napkins. Men are just as happy (if not happier) drinking beer from the bottle as they are from a glass. They don't have to worry which fork to use for the salad and dessert. Trust me on this one.

The same goes for furniture. Men like big, cushy chairs, footrests and coffee tables that they can put their feet up on.

Avoid having too many knickknacks, especially if they're breakable. If your house is too cluttered, it sends the message that you like things more than you like people.

When it comes to decorating, less is more. Leaving space in your house or apartment says you're open to having someone join you. It's subtle, but it's true. You don't have to go all leather or minimalist, but think comfort and casual.

Men Like to Take the Initiative

There is a big difference between being aggressive and being assertive. Men often say they want women to make the first move, but when they do, they act as if they've been attacked by the fifty-foot woman. The truth is, guys are trained to be the initiator in a dating situation. It's like wearing a tie on a ninety-degree day; they may not always like it, but they accept it nevertheless.

You can, however, let a man know that you are available and interested as long as you are subtle about it. This doesn't mean you should walk up to a guy at a party and say, "Date me, you fool." Instead, strike up a conversation with the fellow and if he still doesn't get the hint, give him your business card before you leave. Tell him, "It was great meeting you. Please feel free to give me a ring." This allows the man to make the decision about calling.

Another great way to let a man know you're interested is to let a friend (or the host of a party) inform the guy you're interested in that you wouldn't mind a telephone call. Yes, we used to do this in high school, but it still works for adults! This way the guy can be honest with your emissary about whether or not he's got a girlfriend, whether or not he's interested. It also saves you the humiliation of being rejected in person.

A few years ago, I was working with a producer who was single and available. I knew her well enough to have a good idea of the type of man she liked, and the stage manager seemed to fit the bill.

I took him aside one day and said, "Steve, are you single and open to meeting a woman?" When he said yes, I told him, "I know someone who I think has a lot in common with you. I think you would enjoy her company. If you don't mind, I'd love to set you guys up for a cup of coffee." He was game, and they ended up dating for a long time.

Men Like to Make Plans

Men like to make plans, especially early on in your courting relationship. If you've dropped enough hints (i.e., "I've always wanted to go blading"), your date will know exactly what you like to do.

If he planned your first few outings and they were disasters, but you still want to see the guy again, tell him it's your turn to decide what you'll do. You can take turns planning.

When it's his turn to choose, be adventurous. If he wants to take you to a football game and you hate football, try it once just for the experience. You may end up having fun in spite of yourself. If you're a sports idiot, don't ask too many questions, because it will be like trying to watch *Felicity* with him interrupting every five minutes to ask, "Who is that guy Noel?" It's downright annoying.

If you are still miserable, tell him that he should save his sports outings for the boys. He'll have a lot more fun being with someone who understands what's going on and can talk the talk.

Likewise, when it's your turn to plan, don't suggest a flea market, ballet or chick flick. (See "Men Know How to Set Boundaries" on p. 45.) Take pity on the guy and do something that you think he'll enjoy. If you can't find anything that both of you like doing together, chalk it up to incompatibility.

Men Want Acceptance

John Gray, Ph.D., author of *Men Are from Mars, Women Are from Venus*, observed the following: "Men want to be accepted by women for who they are, and women need to know that what they do or say has value."

This simple truth is the key to understanding how men

think. If you want to win a man's undying affection, let him know that you like him the way he is. If he's a couch potato and you don't have a problem with that, let him know that your pillows are fluffed and ready. If he doesn't have a college education and he works with his hands, make him feel that he doesn't have to have book smarts in order to be intelligent and that his job is worthy of your respect.

Never compromise your wants and needs for the sake of a relationship, however. You must truly love and accept a man for who he is.

Letting a man know that you approve of him and the life he's carved out for himself is one of most endearing things that a woman can do. All men really want is someone who will love and accept them for who they are. They want someone who won't try to change them, and who sees the wonder inside them. A little sex and a hot meal every once in a while would be nice, but basically, acceptance and understanding are the way to a man's heart.

When a man looks for a partner, he's looking for someone who has the same goals in life, whether it's making a million dollars or making babies.

When my friend Trip first got married, his wife wanted him to become an architect. So he set aside his dream of becoming a screenwriter in order to make her happy. But he hated architecture, and her, for pushing him to do something he didn't like. He began to drink and take drugs as a result of his unhappiness.

After getting a divorce, he met Barbara, who was a writer, artist and photographer. They were both extremely creative, and they had similar goals. They wanted to write screenplays. Barbara not only gave Trip permission to pursue what he really wanted to do in life, but she also shared his passion. They've been together ever since.

By being supportive of a man's dreams and goals, even if they differ from your own, you will win his undying affection. Encourage him to talk about his future plans, and brainstorm how he can reach his goals. Show him that you are confident about his ability to succeed.

Men Know How to Set Boundaries

Women tend to have a harder time setting boundaries than men do. Many of us believe that being a couple means doing everything together all the time. We are insulted if our boyfriends don't join us in doing things that we like, because we see compromise as an act of love.

Conversely, a man will tell you exactly what he will or won't do, and he'll have absolutely no problem if you aren't interested in joining him.

While it's true that one must always compromise in relationships, save it for the big issue stuff like whose parents to visit on Thanksgiving or what religion to raise your children.

In other words, if you hate sports and he never misses a game, a man will happily watch football by himself hugging a bottle of beer instead of you. This doesn't mean he loves you any less for hating football, or that he doesn't want to tackle you *after* the game is over. It simply means he likes sports and you don't.

If a man would rather be eviscerated than go to the ballet or flea market, respect that and go with your girlfriends instead. Don't try to force him to do everything you want to do. Treasure that time apart, and use it to do something you enjoy.

Also, you should never hesitate to set your boundaries when it comes to personal space, be it about your friendships, hobbies, or things that make you uncomfortable. Women are taught that nice girls must grin and bear it, but that's another fallacy that's been passed down from generation to generation.

If you're like me and you hate it when men swear or tell dirty jokes, politely tell the offender, "I don't care what you do when you're not with me, but I'd appreciate it if you wouldn't curse while I'm around." It helps if you smile sweetly when you say this.

Some may tell you to lighten up, but most men will feel chagrined and respect your wishes. Don't wag your finger or preach like a church lady. Be polite, but firm.

Men Like History, But Don't Reveal Your Past Too Soon

Confession may be good for the soul, but it's hell on a relationship. I didn't tell my current boyfriend about my past relationships until two years after we started dating.

In spite of what they may tell you, men don't really want to know the full story. (And they sure don't like to tell it!) Guys get jealous and insecure when a woman talks about her past lovers. They are afraid that you'll compare them to your old boyfriends, and they'll wonder how they measure up—pun intended. Show your man that you're an experienced lover, don't tell him!

As women, we like to talk about our relationships, past and present, and we often reveal too much about ourselves too soon. When this happens, many men (no matter how much they may deny it) will pass up the more experienced woman for one who is seemingly more innocent. It helps alleviate some of the performance anxiety that most men have.

Let your date get to know you first before he gets to know your past, especially if you've gone through some rough times. The fact that you filed for bankruptcy or had a nervous breakdown when you were sixteen isn't relevant right now (you're a different person, but it could affect how he feels about you).

Dating Training Film

***When Harry Met Sally* (1989), Rob Reiner, Director**

In *When Harry Met Sally*, Billy Crystal plays Meg Ryan's best *male* friend, the kind of guy you talk to about bad dates and insights about other men. He also happens to be straight, so the sexual tension is only a scratch'n'sniff away. This film is a fine example of why it's great to be friends with a man first before you are lovers. A relationship that takes time to develop and mature is one that will continue to develop and mature once you've tied the knot.

This is especially important if you are cyberdating, because people often reveal much more about themselves when they're not face-to-face. You may feel really close to someone you're chatting with every night at midnight, but he's still a relative stranger. And it's even more important to protect yourself than it is to make a love connection.

The longer you live, the more baggage you have, and sometimes it's better to keep all those emotional suitcases in the closet for a while. Once you've been dating for a while and you've had a chance to get to know (and possibly love) each other, you can begin to tell him your history.

Men Like to Sleep with Their Women Friends

This was the question posed in the movie *When Harry Met Sally*. Can a man and woman be just friends? A man would say no, because if a heterosexual man really likes a woman, he'll want to sleep with her. A woman would say absolutely yes, because she has an easier time separating her mind and body. What women fail to realize is that male friends can make excellent partners, even if you're not sexually attracted to them at first.

The best thing about having a male friend is that you can fall in love with him as a person. This is why I tell women to wait before having sex. Once you get to know someone really well, you start to think of him as a companion rather than as a boyfriend. It allows you to form an emotional bond that is even stronger than the physical.

Ironically, it's the same thing that happens when you're with a man you were once hot for, but the sexual excitement of the early days has worn off. If that man has other qualities that you find attractive, you have a truly solid relationship. You are bonded with each other and you have the same goals and interests. This is the glue that binds a solid relationship together.

Sex can be learned. You can take seminars together. Watch videos. See a sex therapist. There are ways to improve your sex life, even if you think you are not attracted to the man at first.

Some women are afraid of ruining a friendship by having sex with a male friend. This is the risk you take, but it doesn't have to be that way. If you care deeply for him, your friendship can withstand a change in status. You have a history that involves a loving relationship. This is worth holding onto, even if you are ex-lovers.

Men Can Have Sex with the Ex

You go to your high school reunion and run headfirst into your old boyfriend. He looks about the same, save for a few extra pounds and a little less hair. Your heart starts beating a little faster. He's not married, and you're a swingin' single.

All of a sudden, years of growth and sophistication melt away like an ice cube under a heat lamp, and you find yourself giggling like a silly schoolgirl. Do you excuse yourself and run for the punch bowl, or see what develops with the old beau?

If you find yourself attracted to an old boyfriend or ex-husband, you have to approach him as if you are meeting for the first time. What I mean by this is, despite the history, you are both totally new people. Reverting to the person you used to be is essentially living in the past.

It's like exercising. If you haven't run for a year, you have to start slowly and work your way up to where you used to be. If you go too fast, you will risk getting injured. The same goes for relationships.

If your ex appears to be the exact same person he used to be, you will have the exact same problems you had when you were with him years ago. People do mature over time, but unless you knew your ex when he was very young, men do not change all that much.

If you had a bad breakup where he felt burned, chances are he won't be up for a rematch. Most men will not go back to someone who hurt them. Instead, he will make sure that you know how happy he's been without you. If he burned you, let him know that you are better now than you've ever been. Thank him for letting you go and allowing you to grow into the treasure that you are today.

Don't be tempted to rekindle a relationship that was purely based on sex. Having a "for old times' sake" fling will probably be a disappointment. Chances are your memories are better than the thing actually was. Our minds have a way of filtering out the bad stuff and remembering only the good. Like a performer whose time on stage is up, it's always better to leave on a high note.

Men Don't Respond Well to Guilt

Using guilt to manipulate a man into doing things for you will eventually backfire. Sure, he'll feel beholden to you at first, but nine times out of ten he'll end up hating you. No man wants to feel obligated to you. He should want to do things for you because he likes you and wants to make you happy.

By using guilt, you are setting things up for him to dislike you. He'll do what you want, but he'll resent you for it. It's better to reward him for doing the right thing, rather than guilt him into it. Consider this scenario:

Girl: "Would you do me a favor, and stop off at the grocery store for some milk on your way over?"
Guy: "I don't think I'll have time. I'm coming directly from work."
Girl: "Okay, I'll just have to drink my coffee black. The last time I drank my coffee black I felt nauseous."
Guy: "All right, I'll try to pick up some milk."

Or

Girl: "I understand you're working late tonight, but if you bring me a carton of milk, I promise to bring you those cookies you love so much the next time I come over to your place."

When you've got to choose between guilt or reward, reward wins every time.

Men Don't Like Nags

One of the biggest complaints that men have about women is that we nag, nag, nag. Once we get comfortable with a man, we start trying to change him into our idea of the perfect boyfriend. If you want a man to do the dishes, for example, but his mother always did them for him, honey, he's never going to have dishpan hands.

Here's what you do: Make him aware of the problem and then shut up. If he doesn't do it, no amount of nagging is going to help. We all have free will. It's not your place to change him. He should want to pitch in to make your relationship better. If he's not willing to do the things that you find necessary in order to be together, someone else will come along who will. Decide how important having him do the dishes is to you. Figure this out before you move in together or get married. It'll save splitting up the china after you break up.

Men Don't Like Women Who Are Fixated

If a woman has been single long enough, she sometimes gets fixated on the first man who expresses some interest in her. Of course, women who become too fixated on one man will send him running to the hills or to their local police station.

The Pair and a Spare program is designed to prevent any woman from having a fatal attraction. You may like one man better than another, but you must never sit around waiting for him to call or e-mail you. You're out having fun!

You may think it would be nice to have a guy who thinks of nothing but you day and night, but we have a name for people like that—stalkers. And stalkers are scary!

No man is worth this much of your time or energy. If this sounds like you, stop what you're doing and reread the section on my Pair and a Spare strategy. Force yourself to lose his number and e-mail address. Go cold turkey. Get a friend to sponsor you, so you can call her up every time you feel like calling or contacting him.

I've seen many female clients who have this problem. It comes from a basic lack of self-esteem. These women don't feel that they are valuable enough for a man to pursue them. I tell them to do the inner work, and get professional help if need be. A man won't love you more because you are pursuing him.

Men Don't Like Women Who Are Tactless

There's a thin line between being candid and tactless. If you're upset with a man, don't diss him in public. That's tacky. It makes him feel foolish, and you look nasty. Wait until you are alone before you take him down for some offense.

If he shows up at a formal party in sneakers and jeans, for example, he'll probably be embarrassed enough on his own without your pointing out his social gaffe.

I know it's difficult to do, but don't correct his grammar, posture or manners at the table in front of others. Save the critique for later, and say it in a friendly, helpful way. Tell him, "You look so much sexier when you stand up straight like that," or "You probably don't realize you do this, but you sometimes chew with your mouth open."

If possible, enlist one of his friends or siblings to tell him, because he'll only resent you for pointing these things out. Honey, you're not his mother or his elementary school teacher! But you are his friend, and you would tell a girlfriend if she wore an outfit that made her look like a dork.

Men Don't Want to Hear About Your Female Problems

Most men are befuddled by what happens to a woman when she has her period. Can you blame them? Likewise, we are equally amazed by what happens to a man when he gets sexually excited. It's the wonder of nature.

The same goes for those hellish premenstrual days when you are on edge, quick to anger, and puffy as a Macy's Thanksgiving Day balloon. All I can say is, don't talk about your PMS or any other female problem you might be having with a man you're dating. Save it for your OB-GYN and girlfriends.

Men Don't Want to Meet Your Posse Too Soon

I know you're excited about the guy you've been dating, and you want to show him off to all your friends and family. Well, honey, I have one word of advice for you—don't.

Even if you have a wedding to go to and you need a date, don't ask him to go with you until you have started sleeping together. Until you start having sex, a man isn't interested in meeting your friends and family.

Being discreet about the man (or men) you're dating allows you to spend more time together, alone, without the interference of other people's opinions and advice. We all know how some girlfriends can get jealous about our spending less time with them (never drop your girlfriends for a man!), and how they can sometimes find fault when there is none.

The same goes for parents who think no man will ever be good enough for their little girl. This is why you wait until you're absolutely sure he's serious before announcing your relationship to the world.

Women Men Hate

The Rich Bitch

If you're a wealthy woman, don't flaunt your money. Men still need to feel as though they can provide. It's a basic instinct. Making him feel as if he's not worthy of you or unable to take care of you will put the kibosh on this relationship. Avoid the temptation to pay for everything. Let him know that there are other areas where he is well endowed (I'm talking about his heart as much as anything else).

The Enabler

A man will stay with an enabler because she's supporting him in whatever craziness he's doing, but he'll end up hating her for it in the long run.

The bottom line is, you don't want to date an alcoholic, drug addict, gambler or emotional wreck. Being an enabler almost guarantees that you will insinuate yourself into a needy man's life, but I guarantee you that it's not a place you want to be.

The Man Hater

We need to be careful not to let our anger about past boyfriends, husbands or fathers turn us into angry man haters. I assume that if you've bought this book, you actually *like* men, but sometimes our rage at past injustices can seep into our current relationships without our being aware of it.

If you find yourself griping all the time about men, you might be going through a stage, like teenage rebellion. It's important to get the anger out so you can eventually move on. You don't want any pent-up rage coming out after you're married, right?

Men have a radar for man haters in the same way that women can sense if a man is gay or not. Little comments, a curl of the lip, or outright nastiness are some of the clues. Loving men, faults and all, is the first step to Pair and a Spare dating.

Drama Queens

If you are a drama queen, you are the kind of woman who is always in crisis. A man might be attracted at first to a drama queen because of his instinct to try to rescue. But after the fiftieth teary outburst, middle-of-the-night panic call and screaming fit, the drama queen gets old and the man gets out.

The Earth Mother

These are women who need to take care of the world. Men who like to be mothered are attracted to this kind of woman. The problem with the earth mother is that she's so busy taking care of everyone else that she has neglected the man who is closest to her. She also tends to neglect herself, which is equally unattractive to men.

The Control Freak

If a woman is too much of a control freak, she will never be in a satisfying relationship. A control freak will never find anyone who will live up to her expectations. If you are a control freak, you need to learn how to be more flexible and let others make the decisions and, God forbid, do things their way, even if you don't think it's the right way.

The Vainglorious Woman

Men will date women who come in pretty packages, but if there is no substance beneath the fine clothes and lovely face, they will move on. When you open up a beautifully wrapped present, do you save the paper and ribbons? Rarely. What you're really interested in is the gift inside, right?

The vainglorious woman will take three hours before she's ready to go out. She won't let a man touch her hair because he might mess it up. She'll get up an hour before her boyfriend does so he never has to see her without makeup.

The vainglorious woman may seem like she has it all together because she looks so perfect on the outside, but underneath it all she's ready to erupt. It's difficult to get close to this kind of woman, because she is so good at creating a façade. No matter how good she looks, the vainglorious woman has extremely low self-esteem and men sense this, no matter how attractive she may appear on his arm.

Men Like Women Who Eat

Once upon a time women would squeeze themselves into corsets, then girdles in order to create that coveted hourglass figure. We got rid of that pain, but not the desire to be model-thin.

Combine this ideal with a woman's motivation to succeed and feelings of being out of control and you have a recipe for anorexia. Anorexia, in which people starve themselves to control their weight, affects millions of teenage girls and adult women around the world.

If you think that men want to be with skinny women, think again. Yes, the majority of men prefer women who are not fifty pounds overweight, but they don't want to wrap their arms around a skeleton, either.

Men like women who eat. The woman who goes out on a date and picks at her food like a surly three-year-old is not as much fun as a woman who loves good food. Most men like to eat, and they like women who share their passion for food. Food lovers (not gluttons, mind you) tend to be better lovers, because they are lustier and have what the French call *joie de vivre* (joy of life).

If you are anorexic or bulimic, first, seek professional help. What you're doing to your body and your health must come above all. Then, avoid going out to dinner when you first start dating. Go to the movies, a show, a concert, anything that doesn't involve food.

You can go out for cocktails afterward, but if you don't have food in your stomach, order a Virgin Mary instead. The last thing you want is to get drunk on an early date with a guy. Not only will he be unimpressed, but you don't want to lose control and put your safety in jeopardy.

After you've established a trust and bond with your date, you can tell him that you have issues about food.

It's probably best, however, if you put your dating on

hold until you've solved your eating disorder. It's part of your inner work and coming into the world as a healthy, happy individual.

Men Like Women Who Can Be One of the Boys

Being one of the boys can be fun if you're playing on a coed team (a great way to meet guys!). Sure, men like to win, but the notion that a woman has to let a man beat her in a game is ridiculous. Men love women who are competitive and play hard. Their egos are strong enough (or should be) to take a loss or two, and most will even respect you for winning.

But trying to beat a guy for the sake of winning is unnecessary. You are just playing. There's a reason why it's anatomically impossible for women to have pissing contests. And if you're interested in having any kind of relationship with the guy afterward, it may help to remember that.

Men Know How to Protect Themselves

Before you get to know someone, you must always exercise caution. Tell a friend or relative who you are going out with and where you are going *before* the date. Call that person after you return home to let her know that you've gotten back safe and sound.

In fact, my single friends and I call each other regularly just to make sure everything is okay. I've been playing it safe since I was twelve, when my mother used to ask me to tape a note saying who I was with, what time I was going to be back, and the telephone number where I could be reached on the bathroom mirror.

Always meet a first date in a public place, and go your separate ways afterward. (See "First, Second and Third Date Game Plans" on p. 142.) Once you feel secure, you can let him walk or drive you home. Until then, have him walk you only part of the way before you say good night. Never, ever go to his house or apartment, or take him to yours, on the first few dates.

Keep in mind that unless he's someone who has been introduced to you by a friend or relative, he's a stranger. Take the time to get to know him. You'll discover soon enough whether this guy is worth a second date, or even a second conversation. The more you date, the better you'll get at sizing up a man's personality and background quickly.

Dating Training Film

***You've Got Mail!* (1998), Nora Ephron, Director**

This modern remake of *The Shop Around the Corner* is about two people who like each other online, but hate each other in real life. See this movie if you are currently cyberdating. Pay attention to the scene where Tom Hanks and Meg Ryan decide to meet for the first time in an Upper West Side café, and to the lingering courtship that one can have in cyberspace.

Of course, no real cyberdater would wait as long as Meg and Tom did before exchanging photos or talking on the phone. It's only a movie, after all, so we are asked to suspend our disbelief. But don't suspend your good sense when you are dating online. If you've been chatting and e-mailing for more than a month, it's time to speak on the phone. After three months or more, you should make plans to meet F2F (face-to-face). Apply the same safety rules you would if you met through a personal ad, party or blind date.

Men Can Mix Business with Pleasure

Offices are excellent places to meet men, since some people spend more time working than anything else. But it's dangerous for a woman to date her boss because if it doesn't work out, she's the one who'll lose her job. Plus, he'll always be on top in your relationship.

Dating co-workers has also become increasingly more complicated in this era of sexual harassment. If you really like a man who works in your department and the company has a policy against interoffice romances, one of you will have to change jobs. Either that or you will both have to be extremely discreet about your dating.

If there isn't a policy against interoffice romance, go for it, as long as he isn't your boss or assistant. A good way to date a man you are interested in at work is to start by going out as a group. Going out after work with the gang will take the pressure off the two of you. You can even make the first move here by saying, "We're all going to TGIF after work, wanna join us?" You'll get to see how he behaves on a social level, and you'll have your other workmates there as a buffer.

Never leave sexy messages in his in-box or e-mail. Also, some companies have security cameras everywhere, so don't try smooching or Xeroxing your butt in the mailroom.

Even if you are certain that your company doesn't have surveillance, conduct yourself as if it did. Cameras can be hidden in a variety of palces, and it's better to be safe than sorry. A good rule of thumb is never to write, say or do anything that you wouldn't want broadcast over a loudspeaker or TV monitor.

Do not, under any circumstances, tell anyone else about your crush. Nothing spreads faster than office gossip. Keep your personal business to yourself.

Men Should Treat You Like a Business Client

If you are ever tempted to go dutch on a date, I have one word of advice: don't. Men are used to picking up the tab, and they tend to value what isn't cheap or free. A man can always have dinner by himself—it's your company that's valuable, and, to that end, worth paying for.

The only time you should split a date is if you invite him to a formal occasion and he's doing you a favor by accompanying you. That's the sole exception.

Furthermore, the men you are dating should treat you with the respect and care that they would give to a business client. I've noticed that women don't get treasured today, because they don't expect to be treated well anymore.

I've been on dates where I've sat in the car until the man opened the door for me. One guy got all the way into the restaurant before he realized I was still outside.

One of my clients, Mary, is currently dating an extremely wealthy man. I asked her how many times he's brought her flowers or little gifts. "Never," she said.

"Mary, you live a block away from Godiva Chocolates, and there's a flower shop on every corner. What does this tell you about the man you're dating?"

"He's not a flowers and candy kind of guy?" she answered timidly.

Nope. It tells you he doesn't care enough about you to go that extra mile. Darlin', it's not the amount of money that a man spends on you that's important, it's the way he shows you that you're special, or that he's thinking about you.

He doesn't even have to buy you anything. If he's a writer, he can write you a love poem. If he's a carpenter, he can build you a bookshelf. It's not the value of the gift, it's the gift of being valued that's important. I don't care how busy he is, it doesn't take much time to call 1-800-FLOWERS!

Look at it this way. Do you think a man would have his client pay for his or her own meal? Most men would offer the client the sun and the moon if it meant closing the deal.

Likewise, men know the importance of being on time.

A guy would never show up late for work every day and expect to keep his job. If he's running late, he will call and tell his boss that he's on his way. Men who are chronically late for dates and do not call to apologize and explain why they're tardy are dissing you.

Apply the "three strikes, you're out" rule to this behavior. Everyone runs into traffic or gets caught in a meeting now and then, so give him three chances. The third time he makes you wait, he's out of your life. Men know business etiquette. It's time they started remembering their dating etiquette.

Men Operate on a "Need-to-Know" Basis

When you first start dating, you need to learn how to become your own Future Boyfriend Investigator (FBI). You can do this by listening and asking questions. If you don't ask whether he's married, divorced or currently dating someone else, he's not going to volunteer the information. Face it, honey, men operate on a need-to-know basis. If you don't ask, he won't tell.

Still, if you know how to listen carefully and ask the right questions, a man will tell you what you need to know within the first three dates. He'll tell you if he's a commitmentphobe, control freak, woman hater or rogue.

Think of it this way: If you were going to hire an employee, you would interview him, ask him where he's worked before and check his references, right? Why not apply the same techniques to dating? And if you think he's not interviewing you, think again!

Remember the scene from the movie *Diner*, where one of the guys made his girlfriend pass a sports test before he agreed to marry her? This is an exaggerated situation, of course, but there's a germ of truth there about the way men think. (I recommend watching this boy-bonding film for insight into the male psyche.)

Alternate between listening and asking questions so it doesn't seem as if you're reenacting the Spanish Inquisition. And ease your research in slowly. Your third date questions should be more intimate than the ones on your first date.

A first date question might be about his work, friends, roommates, pets, living situation, hobbies and interests. The second date, you can ask him about family and friends. By the third date you can ask future-oriented questions such as: "Where do you see yourself in ten years?"

Ask questions that will reveal if this guy meets the criteria on your nonnegotiable list. Here are some areas you might want to explore:

General health—Do you belong to a gym? or Do you work out?
Religion—(Around Christmas, Hanukkah, Easter and Passover) Are you doing anything special for the holidays?
Living arrangements—Do you have roommates? How long have you lived at your current house/apartment?
Finances—How long have you been at your job? What did you do before this? (Don't infer too much from his clothing; he could have borrowed that Armani suit. Also, guys who are in the computer industry tend to dress down. He could be a millionaire dressed in sneakers and torn jeans.)
Children—Do you like kids?
Age—Where did you go to high school/college? Did you see any concerts back then? What was your favorite group?

Divorces—Why did your last relationship end? (Not a first date question, but important to know if you are getting serious.)
Family relationships—Do you have any brothers or sisters? Do you get along with them? Does your family live nearby? (If he lives 3,000 miles away from his parents, there may be a reason. And if he lives with his mother, you need to know that as well.)
Goals/Interests—Where do you see yourself in five years? Ten years? What are you most passionate about? Where did this interest come from?
Workaholic—What are your hours? Do you work on the weekends?
Alcoholic—Is he ordering beer, wine or shots before dinner? Does everybody, including the bartender, know his name?
Gambler—Have you ever been to Vegas or Atlantic City?
Career—What kind of work do you do? What do you love about it? What about it challenges you the most? What about it frustrates you the most? What is your dream regarding your work?
Self-esteem—What have you done in your life that you're most proud of? What do you consider your biggest failure?
History—What's the best thing that's happened to you in the past year? What's the worst? What was it like growing up in your hometown? What were you like as a child?
Playfulness—What would you do if you didn't have work? What is your dream vacation? (My dream vacation is going to this expensive retreat in upstate New York that I've always wanted to visit. I've never been there, but I'd like to go someday. When I talk about this retreat, the reaction I get from my date determines whether or not we have a future together. If

he says, "That sounds like fun," I know we're on the same wavelength.)
Relationships—What do you consider an ideal relationship?
Education—Were you a good student? Did you like school? Do you ever think about going back?
Politics—Have you ever volunteered for a political campaign? What do you think about the President? What would you do if you were President?

Although you want a man to be open and communicative about his goals, personal history and feelings, beware of the man whose main interest in life is himself. The guy you're dating should be equally curious about you. If he doesn't ask you any questions about what your goals are, frankly, Scarlet, he doesn't give damn.

Conversely, if your date is reserved and getting information is like going on an archeological dig, he's either running on empty or he has something to hide.

When a client tells me she's dating the shy, silent type, I ask her if he has a job and a home. You can't get a job or be out in the world if you don't reveal *something* about yourself. The truth is, if a man wants something badly enough, he'll go out and get it. Silence is a way of closing yourself off from people. If he's too quiet, maybe it's better that you leave well enough, and him, alone.

Men Who Don't Call After the First Date Aren't Interested

If a man doesn't call you after your date to either thank you or ask you out for another one, he doesn't want a second date. He may call you a week or two later to see if you're available, but he doesn't really care if you say yes or no.

Let's say a man goes on a sales call; he gets the customer interested in the product he's selling, and then he disappears. Even if he follows up with a call a few weeks later, chances are the customer will have lost interest.

It's the same thing with dating. A man has to follow up in order to close the deal. Not following up after a first date is a sure sign that he isn't interested, or that he's seeing other women.

Why Men Call

- **You're pretty.** Yes, they're *that* superficial.
- **You laughed at his stories.** Or if you didn't, you told some good stories of your own.
- **You touched him.** Not there, but on his hand, shoulder or arm. Hooking onto a man's arm while you walk down the street tells a man you are interested. Maybe you straightened his tie, or gave him a peck on the cheek.
- **You made him feel special.** Somehow during the course of the night, you made him feel good about himself. You were impressed by his mastery of his business, or by his goals in life.
- **You let him know you're interested.** You'd be surprised how many women forget this crucial part of a good date. Let him know, subtly, that you would like him to call. Say something like, "I've been wanting to see that movie for weeks!" or "I've always wanted to go mountain climbing." Whatever it is you want to do, tell him without asking him out. Give him some ideas for your next date.

If a man really likes you, he'll call you within two days. Give him up to a week, because he might be busy with business or family obligations. After that, he's probably not going to call, so let him go. This is why you always have a Pair and a Spare—so you're not just sitting around.

This doesn't mean that you shouldn't go out with him again if he calls a few weeks later. Be aware that he's simply dating like a man, which means he's dating other women. And you should, too. But if you do go out with him, be aware that you are not the top priority in his life. Keep your eyes wide open and your telephone buzzing with other calls.

If a guy doesn't call and he's hard to get a hold of, he doesn't want to be reached. When a man is serious about a woman, he'll give her all his digits, including his home, work, cell, e-mail and fax numbers. Girlfriend, if the boy really likes you, he'll give you the numbers off his high school jersey. If a guy only gives you his cell phone number, it means he wants to stay mobile.

Women, on the other hand, need to maintain their privacy for their own protection. If you're dating a Pair and a Spare, I suggest using a different number from your home or work. It can be a service number or a separate phone line. If you have a cell phone, do what the boys do and use that number. If you have a computer, give him your e-mail address, and keep one screen name for dating purposes only.

These days, anyone with Caller ID can see your phone number. When you do call a guy you don't know very well from your home or office (which I don't recommend), disable his Caller ID by pressing *67 before dialing his number. Wait until you have the 411 on the guy you're dating before you give him your private number.

Men Have Their Own Holidays

Holidays are emotional events for women. They are tied to our family histories, past experiences and future expectations. Men, in general, don't like holidays and see them as just another day on the calendar. They resent being manipulated into buying gifts or spending more money than they normally would to go out to eat.

If you understand this about men, you won't feel so bad when they don't share your enthusiasm during the holidays. Don't choose Valentine's Day or New Year's as the litmus test for how much a man cares about you. Most men, if they were to tell you the truth, would say that Valentine's Day is a Hallmark Holiday and New Year's is for amateurs.

If he forgets to buy flowers or candy on February 14th, it doesn't mean he's not interested in you. And if he won't wear a pointed hat or spend hundreds of dollars on subpar food on New Year's Eve, it doesn't mean he's not interested in you. However, if the man you're dating sticks around from Thanksgiving until New Year's, he's *definitely* interested.

Beware of the man who disappears during the holidays and reappears afterward. He's telling you he's either cheap, married or not committed enough to share an event that is meaningful to you.

Men have their own holidays. The high holy days for guys are the Super Bowl, World Series, NBA playoffs, Stanley Cup, World Cup, heavyweight championships, Master's, Grand Prix and the Kentucky Derby. I know I left out a few, but you get the idea. It's best if you acknowledge these days with the same spiritual reverence that you might reserve for Mother's Day, birthdays and anniversaries.

You can celebrate these male holidays by helping him and his friends consume the traditional food such as beer, chips, chili, hot dogs and burgers. Do not pick this time to talk to him about your relationship or anything important. Let him bond with the boys. (You will gain extra points for this.)

You can also *teach* your man about the holidays and events that mean a great deal to you. Don't expect him to think of this on his own or to read your mind. Give him at least a week's notice that the day is approaching. Tell him exactly what it is you would like him to do.

Tell him, for example, "Valentine's Day is coming up next week. We should probably make a reservation now." Or, "Our one-year dating anniversary is coming up. I've already picked out your present."

That's about as subtle as you can be without writing in his appointment book: "Buy me flowers today!" There's nothing wrong with planning that day for the both of you. He will be eternally grateful.

And don't be insulted if your date doesn't have a clue about how to celebrate one of your female holidays. It's more important to see how he treats you on the other days of the year.

If you're alone on the holiday you love, get together with your girlfriends and talk about how much you love men. Rent a romantic chick flick like *Sleepless in Seattle*. Don't get caught up in man-hating bitch sessions, because they create the wrong kind of energy that will stay with you after you leave. Celebrate love, don't revile it.

While you're at it, why not celebrate the holidays that are important to men, too? Go to a sports bar and watch the World Series with a group of friends. You might meet someone there, but don't expect the men to pay attention to anything else but the TV. My co-author, Jodie, was writing an article about an upscale strip club in New York during the baseball playoffs, where she witnessed the men telling a beautiful, half-naked dancer to move away from the big screen so they could watch the game! Get the picture?

Men Know How to Let Go

When a woman burns a man he will curse her, go out drinking with his friends and, eventually, move on. He may hurt for a while, but he'll chalk it up to experience. He'll tell himself that there are better women waiting for him in the wings.

When a woman gets dumped, she will hold on to her bitterness and curse all mankind. Some men do this too, of course. We call them misogynists. These are the guys that end up on *Cops* or eating a can of beans at a YMCA.

Here's what you can do if you find yourself feeling bitter about your past relationships. Instead of focusing on all the bad things that happened to you, figure out what lessons that relationship taught you. The more you focus on the bad things your ex did, the harder it is to let go. Believe it or not, once you get past the pain and anger, you will find the jewel that your ex has left you.

Women who constantly complain about how the men in their lives have treated them badly are telling their future partners that this is the way they are used to being treated, and the way they will talk about him. A man will never know how to treat you unless you tell him.

You must also learn how to forgive. Every encounter is like a stepping stone that will get you closer to where you want to be as an individual, and to who you want to be with.

There's a big difference between the way men and women deal with letting go. This is a visual concept, so imagine what I'm about to tell you and you'll be able to *feel* the difference.

Women hold onto relationships for dear life (visualize hands clenched in a fist). Men are more open about relationships (imagine two open palms). Now, which way can you hold more, with open hands or with clenched fists? There are so many more possibilities when you are open and, if necessary, willing to let go. If a relationship isn't working for whatever reason, don't waste your time and his trying to fix it.

Relationships are like homework assignments. We are assigned people from whom we can learn valuable life lessons. When a person leaves, it means the assignment is over and it's time to move on to the next lesson. If necessary, write down what you've learned about yourself after every breakup.

Is there a pattern with each man you've dated? Negativc patterns in relationships are like being left back in school to repeat a grade. There are clearly lessons still left to be learned. If you don't, you will never graduate to a healthier relationship.

Once you've discovered the lesson you need to learn from the person you were with, you can move on to the next level of commitment in your next relationship. Women who don't take the time to examine these lessons, and jump from man to man, will repeat the same mistakes with all the men they meet. Guaranteed.

If your lesson was to learn how to be with a man you don't have to take care of, good—you won't find yourself attracted to that kind of man again. And if you do, the red flags will come out and stop you from taking that relationship any further. You are poised for your next experience, which, with any luck, will be better than the last one.

EXERCISE: "RELATIONSHIP SELF-ESTEEM"

If you are in a relationship now that is not making you happy, write down all the things that bother you about your boyfriend. Be as specific as possible. Let's say your boyfriend has trouble communicating, he lies to you or he has difficulty expressing his anger. Break these down even further. "My boyfriend doesn't like to talk about his feelings. He tells me he's working late when he's going out with his pals. He yells at me whenever I disagree with him."

Now ask yourself if you are suppressing any feelings. Are you lying to yourself about something? What are you angry with yourself about?

Chances are that you'll find the problems in your relationship directly reflect the problems that you are having in your own life. There are no coincidences when it comes to choosing a partner.

Instead of trying to change your boyfriend, concentrate on solving the issues in your own life. The relationship will either get stronger or dissolve entirely.

You might find that you need some time to yourself. This is why men say, "I can't deal with my stuff and her stuff, too."

Men Keep Their Private Dramas to Themselves

For the most part, and I'll grant you there are exceptions, men don't sit around complaining about their lives. (They don't call it "bitching" for nothing.) Men are more action-oriented. When they get a minor injury playing sports, for example, their teammates or coach usually tell them to walk off the pain. No time for whimpering.

Most guys don't like to draw other people into their dramas. Men take care of their personal business discreetly. If a man has something serious going on, he'll withdraw from the world until he's taken care of it. Women, on the other hand, feel the need to share their personal hell with everyone. As women, we need to realize that there are times when we should step back and take care of ourselves.

Only after you've dealt with your problem should you come out and talk about it. Blabbing about your financial, emotional or physical problems will send men fleeing. If you *must* tell someone, talk to a therapist, clergyman, girlfriend or family member. Or you can try writing in a journal, which is the next best thing to telling someone.

If you have an ongoing problem such as a chronic illness or phobia, keep it to yourself until you've dated someone for several months. Remember, your goal is to have fun and keep things light and casual. Wait until the man you're dating becomes a close friend before taking the skeletons out of the closet. There will be plenty of time to swap secrets later on.

How to Stay Single Forever

Women do so many things to sabotage themselves when they are dating. If you are doing any of the following, you are increasing your chances of staying single forever.

1. **Refuse to let go of your past**. Do you ever wonder why men can do heinous things and come back a few years later as new men, accepted and even respected by the people who once reviled them? Richard Nixon is an excellent example of this reincarnation. He was forced to resign from office for crimes that were committed at the Watergate Hotel. After a brief hiatus from the public eye, he reemerged as an elder statesman and eminence grise. Ted Kennedy is another politician who was able to put tragedy behind him. There's absolutely no reason why this can't be the case for a woman scorned.

Women who are ashamed of their past, for whatever reason, often select men who are inappropriate, unavailable or unwilling to commit. I have a client named Sarah who has totally changed her life. She's dropped about fifty pounds, which helped transform the way she thinks about herself.

The problem is, Sarah still feels unworthy of love. When she was heavier, she would behave promiscuously, often sleeping with men she didn't know. She thought that was the only way she could be with a man.

I asked her, "What's stopping you from being the beautiful, vivacious woman that you are today?" She said, "I still believe this is what men expect of me." I asked Sarah if she was still hanging out with the same type of men. She was. "I guess I feel I'm not worthy of having a decent man because of what I did in the past."

Once you've gone through a major change in your life, you have to be able to shed your past and start again as if you were reborn.

Ten years ago I decided to change my name to Myreah Moore (my real name is Myra Stringer) because I realized that my old name did not fit the person I felt I had become. I had a little funeral for my old self and adopted my new name and persona. I felt that my parents and my peers did not support who I really was. My last name, Stringer, made me feel as if I was being strung along.

Even though this worked for me, you don't necessarily have to change your name in order to change your life. Sometimes moving away to a new city can allow you to start over. No one will have preconceived notions of who you are.

Once you're where you want to be, you can return home and reintroduce yourself. Don't let anyone try to set you back by relating to you the way you used to be. Tell them, "That was the old me. This is who I am now."

A good way to recreate yourself is to have a mentor or role model. Study that person so you can discover what it is that makes her so admirable or successful.

If you want to look a certain way, cut out a picture of the woman you'd like to emulate and bring it to a hairstylist. Remember, this is just a guideline because photos in magazines are heavily airbrushed, so even the models and actresses don't really look that good in real life. Also, if your hair is bone-straight, you're never going to have naturally wavy locks. A good hairstylist can find the right cut for your particular hair.

If you're saying, "I like myself just the way I am," good for you! But ask yourself if the person you are right now is getting dates. Are you getting compliments on the way you look? Do people like being around you? Change doesn't have to be forever. If you try out something that doesn't work, you can always go back to your old self again.

I have a client whose idol is Susan Sarandon. I've asked her to break down the qualities Sarandon possesses that she admires. Now she's working on being more powerful, politically active, and self-assured as she ages. Her goal, as a divorced woman, is to be in a committed relationship without being married. Every time I see my client now, she has more of an inner glow.

2. Spend all your time with gay men. Like surrounding yourself with cats, single women often seek out gay men for companionship—and they are wonderful confidants. Gay men are fun to be with because you can gossip, shop and talk about other men. In addition to being a great source of information about men in general, they will also be honest with you about the guys you're dating.

The problem is, gay men are the Prince Charmings we all dreamed about as children. They dress well, they're good-looking and they're sensitive to our needs. Women have to see their gay friends for what they are: another girlfriend. They are not your surrogate boyfriends.

Don't hang out with your gay friends exclusively because you'll cut off other men who might be interested in you. If another man sees you out with a guy, he's not going to approach you because he might think you're already attached.

When I was a little girl, I had an uncle who turned out to be a drag queen. He taught me how to apply makeup, dress up and walk in heels. He was my charm school, but he sure as hell wasn't the man I wanted to be with when I grew up.

3. Become a paranoid city dweller. Women who live in cities always complain about how hard it is to connect with men. Even the most sophisticated men are put off by women who are cold, distrusting of strangers and put on airs like elitist snobs. You don't have to be a rube in order to be friendly.

Since many people who live in big cities come from other places anyway, it's your job to be that small-town girl in the big city. You can't be afraid to talk to people you don't know. If you don't do this, you will stay disconnected (i.e., single) forever.

If you're living in an apartment building and you don't know at least three of your neighbors, you are doing something wrong. Get to know your doorman, if you have one, and ask him to keep an eye out for single men in the building. The same for your butcher, dry cleaner or personal trainer. Talk to the people in your laundry room. Join the tenants' association (or form one).

Statistics have shown that most people marry someone who lives within a ten-block radius. If a single man moves into your building, become the Welcome Wagon. You don't have to bake him a cake (that will frighten him), but you can introduce yourself and offer your help if he needs information on finding the best local shops or restaurants.

Have a regular place in the neighborhood that you go to. It can be a coffee shop (think *Seinfeld* and *Friends*), restaurant or gym. Once you become a regular, people will recognize you, say hello when you pass in the street and refer you to eligible men. Walk your dog in the park, and talk to the other dog walkers. Have a party and invite your neighbors.

If you are religious, find out where your local church or synagogue is. If not, get yourself a tattoo. Whatever you do, don't sit at home with Ben & Jerry. Get out of the apartment.

4. Complain constantly about being single. Whiners are annoying. Everybody has dry spells, so there's nothing wrong with you if you haven't had sex in long time. You are still an active, viable person. And stop talking about the losers you've dated.

5. Date a man on the rebound. If a man has just broken up with his wife or girlfriend, he is probably not ready to date, much less move in with you. Men who can't be by themselves need mothers, not lovers. Tell the rebounder to check back with you in three months. Give him time to mourn his loss, try to win back his ex, fail and then get over it. Unless he goes through this process, he won't be ready, and any relationship he does get into will be fraught with disaster.

6. Have long-distance relationships. Nowadays, with so many women cyberdating, it's not uncommon to fall for a man who lives 3,000 miles away. Long-distance relationships can work because they force you to prolong the courtship, which gives you time to learn more about each other before you get serious. I have a long-distance relationship with my honey, and I like it that way.

But if your goal is to wake up every morning with someone on the other side of bed, then LDRs are not for you. LDRs mean you will spend a few days in his city, he spends a weekend in yours and you end up spending lots of money on phone calls and time in airports.

This kind of relationship is ideal for many men. They get to have their own place, their own territory even, and they don't have to make room for a hair dryer, moisturizer bottles and pantyhose. If you're like me and you're comfortable having a half-continent of personal space, great. If not, one of you has to pick up stakes and move, and nine times out of ten it's going to be the woman.

Don't do anything drastic (i.e., cancel your cable) until you've spent at least six months in the same city. It's the day-to-day stuff that can sometimes put a stake through the heart of a relationship.

7. Have too many cats. I love animals too, but having too many cats (a fave among women) will frighten a man, who is probably a dog person anyway. Plus, you're at risk of slouching toward eccentricity, and you're probably too young to be called "the cat lady" by your neighbors.

I do have a friend who swears that her cat Simon knows better than anyone if a man is a good person. When Simon throws up on a man's shoes, he's not probably not worth a second date. Whatever you may think about what Simon says, limit your menagerie to two or three.

8. Have too many children. If you have six children from different men, you've got to get yourself to Planned Parenthood right away. Children need money, attention and love. Men need money, attention and love, and you need money, attention and love. If you have to choose, the children are going to come first every time. It's important to wait until you're positive the man you're with is in it for the long run before you have kids.

9. Talk about your biological clock. Go ahead–tell him about how you cry every time a stroller goes by. The fact that a man can practically father a baby and be wished a "Happy Birthday" by Willard Scott at the same time is one of the great inequities of life.

The good news is that fertility treatments are making it possible for women to have children later in life. Don't panic; if you want a baby badly enough, there are ways. And you don't even need a living, heavy-breathing man beside you to do it anymore.

Besides, not every woman on earth is meant to have a child. And if you do happen to meet the man of your dreams after your clock has stopped ticking, there are plenty of children who need loving adoptive parents.

10. Have a nervous tic. While hair-twisting is an excellent flirting technique, doing it until you need Rogaine is a neurosis alarm. The same goes for nervous tapping, nail-biting, fidgeting and blinking. If you suffer from any of these tics, you are probably not quite ready to date. Do some more inner work to find out what's at the root of your hair-pulling (sorry for the pun).

If it's something that you will probably never stop, or it turns out, God forbid, that you have Parkinson's, be up front about it in a casual way. Say, "You know Michael J. Fox? We both have Parkinson's, so my hand sometimes shakes a little."

Make a joke about it: "It really helps me when I'm on the dance floor." Or simply say, "It's been a while since I've dated, and I'm a bit nervous." If he really likes you, he won't give a hoot if you have a little tremor.

11. Try to enlist him in your cult. If you're waiting to hitch a ride on a comet, you probably aren't dating anyone outside your zany little world anyway. Plus, you won't be around for too much longer.

12. Have a weird girlfriend. We all have one. We love her to death, but she's a killer when you're not one-on-one. Maybe she giggles like a hyena, hates men, or dresses like a bag lady. The good news is that men also have weird friends they hide from you.

Weird girlfriends are like family—you should wait before you introduce them to the man you're serious about. A solid relationship can handle loose cannons. A relationship where the jury is still out may not. Your friends are a reflection of who you are, so you are exposing a bit of your own strangeness by allowing him to meet your whacked-out gal pals.

If you're a constant complainer, a good way to stop yourself is to ask friends to point out every time you start to bitch. Whenever you catch yourself whining, put a dollar in the kitty. Not only will you become aware of how much you complain, but you'll probably stop before you amass enough cash to buy a blue-chip company. Once you've successfully kicked the complaining habit, you can also reward yourself with a massage or a new dress.

Men Don't Want to Be Bought

Never buy a gift for a man when you first start dating, because he'll feel as though you're trying to buy his affection. If it's his birthday or a holiday, send him a card or a trinket. Once you get further along in the relationship, you can get him something meaningful.

One of my clients told me that she met a man at a party whom she liked a lot. He offered to give her a lift home afterward. Although she refused the ride (good move), she was so grateful for the gesture that she bought him flowers the next day. The man never called her again.

The next time she saw him (they had a friend in common), he 'fessed up and told her that the flowers put too much pressure on him. Now that's a communicative guy! His rationale: If she's going to give him flowers for offering a ride home, what is she going to do for a dinner and a movie?

Honey, *you* are the one who should be getting the flowers, not him. A man doesn't expect or even want to get gifts from a woman he's wooing. Let him do the courting, so keep your credit card in your purse.

Men Know How to Lose

Boys learn early on that it's okay to lose. Once again, it harkens back to those early days of playing sports. Where do you think the saying "No pain, no gain" came from?

Women have a hard time losing. Since they blame themselves for everything, losing is proof that they just can't hack it. Winning becomes less important than not failing again. And when it comes to relationships, women see every failure as a personal loss.

Men, on the other hand, know that when you're playing a game, any game, someone has to lose. If you happen to be on the losing end that day, you play the tapes back, think about the wrong moves you might have made, and use that knowledge to play a little bit differently (and hopefully smarter) the next time.

When you fail at something (and everyone does at one time or another), you are also opening the door to a future opportunity and future success.

When some women are in a failed relationship, they often go back to the same kind of man again and again because we're afraid to try something new. Some of us are determined to get it right, but others gravitate toward the hurt we know rather than open ourselves up to the hurt we don't know. In this case, familiarity breeds comfort, not contempt.

The fact is, honey, every time a relationship fails, it's fate's way of telling you there is someone out there who wants you more. When I ask my female clients why they think a relationship has ended, nine out of ten will tell me it was their fault.

In contrast, men will tell me, "It just didn't work out," or "She wasn't the one." They don't blame themselves, or go into emotional analysis about who did what to whom. They pick themselves up and get right back out there.

The problem is that most women don't look at men's failings, they look for their own: "Maybe I talked too much, nagged too much, or didn't talk enough." They twist themselves into neurotic pretzels in order to change themselves for the next relationship.

There's a philosophy salesmen use when making a pitch: Some will. Some won't. Some can't. So what? Next. This is the same philosophy that you should use when dating. Some will date you. Some won't. Some can't. So what? Next.

A failed relationship gives us information that we can use in our journey. Every man you break up with tells you something about the kind of man you want in your future. Learn from that.

If you continue to blame yourself for failed relationships, take a few deep breaths to clear your head and repeat the salesman's mantra. If your friends or family ask you what went wrong, shrug your shoulders and say, "He just wasn't the one."

If you look at the way men compete, you'll see that they play to win. But they also know that they don't have to destroy their opponent in order to be victorious. As women, we are brought up to believe that we must compete with other women for attention, compliments and, of course, men. We feel the only way to win is to put down our competition.

The truth is, the only one you need to compete with is yourself. Look at what Muhammad Ali did before a fight. It wasn't what he said about his opponent that made him so unusual.

What Ali did that was so brilliant was to tell anyone who'd listen how he was the greatest fighter of all time; he talked about how he danced like a butterfly and stung like a bee. He pumped himself up so much that even if the other guy was stronger or faster, he lost whatever edge he may have had walking into the ring. The perception became the reality.

Men, in general, believe there is more than enough room for all of us to be heroes. It's not just the pitcher or the quarterback who can win the game—anyone at any time can make the winning play. The weakest man on the team can intercept the ball and take it through the goalposts. Everybody's a player.

Women have more trouble understanding what it's like to be a team player. We have adopted what I call the bride's philosophy when it comes to competitors. The unspoken rule is that no one can look better than the radiant bride. Why do you think all the bridesmaids are made to wear those freakishly ugly dresses? A truly confident woman will allow her bridesmaids to look as lovely as she does. (Note that the ushers all wear the same thing as the groom does. When you're a team, everybody wins!)

Men Know It's Okay to Be Cocky

Even the word *cocky* exudes maleness. How many times have you heard a man say something like, "I can bench-press twice my body weight," "I made millions in the stock market last year," or, "I sold more ad space than anyone in my department"?

These declarations may seem like bragging, but no one faults a guy for being proud of his accomplishments. Now imagine a woman saying the same thing. Would you think she was an arrogant bitch?

This double standard exists because men are rewarded for their bravado. They also know that it's impossible to have everyone like them. It's not even desirable! If you don't care about what others may say about you, you will find it easier to make bold, even seemingly boastful statements.

Women have been brought up to be self-effacing. When we see other women who are self-confident, we accuse them of being arrogant. We want to knock them down a few pegs. When we see an arrogant man, the same women who say "Who does she think she is?" will think "Hmmm, he must be special."

Unbridled arrogance can clear a room faster than a fire alarm. But there's nothing wrong, in my opinion, with being a diva. I consider myself the diva of dating. Being a diva means you are opinionated. You have every right to demand respect. So what? It's better than being a doormat. Men walk all over doormats. Women need to encourage each other to be larger than life.

If you're good at something, don't be afraid to let other people know about your talent. If you can't think of a single thing you're good at, honey, you've got some work to do. Everyone is good at *something*. Figure out what you enjoy doing, and learn how to do it well.

Men Know How to Break Up

When a man breaks up with a woman, he will take her to a public place where she can't make a scene. He will tell her straight up that the relationship isn't working, or that he's found someone new.

If you're following my Pair and a Spare program, you will also find yourself dating men who are incompatible with you. When that happens, go to a public place and be as candid as possible without hurting his feelings.

You might say, for example: "I like you as a person, but I don't think we make a good couple. I think it's best if both moved on." If he starts to argue with you, tell him, "There's probably fifty other women who would like to have you as a boyfriend; I'm just not one of them." You'll be amazed by how quickly he'll agree with you.

Tell him the truth (or get as close to the truth as you can without being mean). A man will respect you so much more than if you said, "Let's be friends" or that perennial favorite, "It's not you, it's me." If you truly want to be his friend, fine. If not, don't cop out by telling every man you break up with that you want to be his pal. Baby, you don't have time for that!

Disappearing or never taking his phone calls is also a copout. As you know from the Pair and a Spare strategy, this will only make him more ardent in his pursuit of you. Women are so afraid of hurting a guy's feelings that they will go to any length not to tell him the truth. We are also frightened of confrontation because we can't bear the thought of being disliked. A man, on the other hand, will tell it like it is: "I felt trapped," or "I'm not ready to be monogamous."

This is the way men sever a business deal gone sour. They say, "This isn't working. No hard feelings." Sure, there are the cowards who tell you they'll call when they have no intention of doing so. Isn't it worse to have someone you're dating lead you on, rather than tell you straight out that it isn't working? Always date with integrity. This way you won't have to hide in the shadows should you ever run into your ex again.

Men Don't Give Too Much

I know some people cringe at the word *selfish,* but I don't believe that being a selfish dater is a bad thing. As girls, we are socialized not to think of ourselves, and to put others' needs first. Putting yourself first allows you to give more to other people because you won't feel deprived. You've already given to yourself, so you won't depend on others to make you happy.

Men do whatever it takes to make themselves happy. It's in a woman's nature to be a caregiver, so she often puts other people's needs first. This is a wonderful trait, but single women shouldn't forget to take care of themselves.

The woman who puts her boyfriend through medical school doesn't always end up with a doctor. The woman who makes personal sacrifices for her boyfriend is not guaranteed that he will reciprocate in kind.

Being a selfish dater means making sure that your needs are met. Is he picking you up at a convenient time or place? Are you doing something that you enjoy? Do you feel safe? Is he being courteous and respectful?

I always tell my clients: When you're dating, never do for a man what he can hire someone else to do for him. Don't cook for him (unless you *really* like to cook), don't clean his house, don't do his laundry. Honey, you are not his mother and you are not his maid. You'll also set a bad precedent should you ever get married. If you're both working outside the home, these household chores should be shared.

If he asks you to be the hostess at his party, suggest that he call a caterer instead. This way you can mix and mingle like an equal partner. Don't clean up afterward. He'll be grateful to you, but he won't respect you. And he will *expect* you to do it the next time, and next time, and the next.

Women often think, "If I go out of my way for him, he'll be appreciative." Or they think, "The nicer I am to him, the

The Ex-Files Quiz

How do you know when it's time to let go?

1. Do you find yourself making lame excuses like "My cat needs me" when he asks you out?
2. Do you start flirting shamelessly with waiters and delivery-men?
3. Did you "forget" his birthday?
4. Do you find yourself daydreaming about a solo vacation to Cancun?
5. Did you get a promotion because of all the extra time you're spending at work?
6. Did you recently install Caller ID?
7. Did you change your screen name?
8. Have you taken to killing large bugs and lifting heavy objects yourself?
9. Are your girlfriends telling you to "dump the bastard"?
10. Is he starting to remind you of your other ex-boyfriends?

If you answered yes to five or more of the questions above, it's time for you to ex-terminate your relationship.

nicer he'll think I am." Sorry, but it doesn't work that way. Be nice to *yourself*. Men respect women who respect themselves, and that means setting the boundaries for what you will and won't do for him.

It's not the fifties anymore, honey, so men don't marry women for their cooking or homemaking ability. If you want to cook for him, make him promise to return the favor by making you a meal or taking you out to a fine restaurant (I'm talkin' real linen on the table, and waiters who aren't wearing paper hats).

Don't make the mistake of being too nice. I learned this lesson the hard way. When I was younger, I used to think that if I did things for the guys I was dating, they'd like me more. I would even write thank you notes after a first date. That was just the way I was raised. But instead of liking me more, the boys would get terrified and run away.

I remember one guy in particular named Zachary, who called me and asked, "Why did you send this note to me?" When I told him that I was simply thanking him for a lovely evening he said, "You don't have to thank me for the date! What do you expect me to do now?" It made him feel as if he had to do even more for me the next time we went out. Of course, there was no next time.

Unfortunately, I didn't learn from this experience, because I would continue being too nice to all my dates, until one day a guy finally told me what I was doing wrong. He explained to me why men want spice more than they want nice.

The moral of this story is, don't give too much too soon. The guys are the ones who are doing the courting, not the other way around. At the end of a date, a gracious thank you is quite enough.

Men Are Opinionated

Although a man will sleep with a woman who has been lobotomized if she also has blonde hair, long legs and big boobs, smart men don't like bimbos, and even those who do don't like them for long. So the days of keeping your opinions to yourself, laughing disingenuously at his jokes or pretending to be fascinated when he discusses gigabytes or something equally eye-glazing are over.

Intelligent men prefer women who are a challenge and, therefore, just as opinionated as they are. Tell him you think he's full of crap if his political theories don't match your own, or if he happens to tread into an area that you know a lot about. I've always believed that men love candor. You can have separate ideas and still be equals.

If you find that he's the type of guy who never wants to lose an argument, lose him. If he screams at you when you disagree with him, he'll probably scream at you when you fight about real issues. If he calls you an idiot, call a cab.

Arguing (in the true sense of word) can be an excellent way to get information about another person. Pay attention when he lets his guard down, and when he puts his gloves up. What are his hot button issues? Can he agree to disagree? But most important, can he let you be right when you are?

A debate should be like a seesaw—sometimes he's up and sometimes you are. If you haven't been able to say a word in thirty minutes, he's got power issues. If you find yourself thinking about what happened at work while he's talking, you need a better conversationalist. One-sided discussions are nothing more than verbal masturbation.

Having opinions but being open to hearing the other side is a sign of true self-confidence. Women who are afraid to speak up do not value themselves. You should never feel intimidated when talking to someone who you believe is smarter than you; information is one of the greatest gifts that anyone can give you. If you happen to be smarter than your date, never dumb yourself down in order to make the guy feel more comfortable.

I do believe, however, that long-term relationships work best when two people are on approximately the same level of intelligence. The Pygmalion story about the older, smarter, patrician metamorphosing the female student into a socially acceptable butterfly seems wonderful on the surface, but it's actually an insidious fairy tale. Eventually, one or both of the players feels resentful or mismatched.

Unless *you've* reinvented yourself or you are a self-made woman, the man who tutored you will at some point throw your past right back in your face.

Dating Training Film

Diner (1982), Barry Levinson, Director
Although this film is set in 1959, the boy-bonding theme still holds true today. *Diner* involves a group of college guys who have been buddies since childhood. They still hang out together, most notably at a local diner, where they talk about women, sports and other locker room topics.

Rent this video for insight into the kind of friendships that men form, and why women have to honor them in order to keep the peace. One funny subplot has the young Steve Guttenberg giving his fiancée a sports quiz as a prerequisite to marriage. If she doesn't score high enough, the wedding is off! The truth is, you don't have to be a sports fanatic in order to win a man's heart, as long as you give him some private game time with the

Men Don't Like Wimps

Men who can control you will eventually leave you or make you so miserable that you leave them. He's not your boss and he's not your father, so don't put up with taking orders.

If a man doesn't trust you, he doesn't trust himself. If he needs to know where you are and what you're doing at all times, he doesn't trust himself. This is a major red flag. If he accuses you of sleeping with someone else, chances are he is sleeping with someone else, or is thinking about cheating on you.

Overprotective or possessive men are projecting their own inner demons onto you. This is not cute, nor is it evidence of his great love for you. This kind of jealousy can be dangerous, and it will only get worse after you're married. It can even be a precursor to abuse. When your boyfriend asks you where you were, tell him and end it there. If that doesn't satisfy him, leave him—immediately.

Don't mistake jealousy for caring. Any man who needs to dominate a woman does not respect her. It means that he feels weak and that the only way that he can feel powerful is to control someone else.

Real men don't like wimps. In fact, the more powerful the man, the more he will seek out women who are not cowed by him. Take the young Frank Sinatra, for example. He could have any woman in the world, and he nearly did. He didn't stay with his first wife, who also happened to be the mother of his children, because she had Old World values. She was taught that women should never question their husbands.

The love of his life was Ava Gardner, not because she was the most beautiful, but because she was tough, headstrong and opinionated. She matched him point for point. They fought like Ninjas, and he loved her for it.

Think of it this way: Would you want a man who did everything you told him to do? Honey, you might enjoy the power at first, but after a while, you'd lose respect for him and fall for the first man who told you where to get off.

Men Don't Like Princesses

We all want to feel like a princess sometimes. It's nice to have men wait on us and grant our every wish with the wave of our imaginary magic wand. Well, baby, men don't like princesses because they don't believe in fairy tales.

Look what happened to Princess Diana. Princess Diana was beautiful and royal, but it was the commoner Camilla who won the Prince's heart. She may not be a beauty, but there is something in her that made Prince Charles feel important, wanted and loved.

There are too many expectations placed on women who want to be on a pedestal. They aren't human. Men like women they can talk to and be themselves with. Once you place yourself on that pedestal, you are setting yourself up to be dethroned.

Men Don't Like Women Who Are Wild

One of the biggest mistakes women make is talking about sex too soon. Women may think that men like it when they bring up sex, but men actually think that women who talk dirty are easy, even if they are turned on. They see it as a sign that you want to sleep with them. If you don't follow through, you are nothing but a tease, and men hate teases.

Never grind on the dance floor with a man you've just met. That makes you look cheap and low-class. Dirty dancing is fun when you're with someone you know and like, but a stranger? No way. If you're rubbing up against him on the dance floor, you're telling him that you want to have sex later.

Don't drink too much when you're trolling for men. If you know you can't handle liquor, know when to stop. Guys aren't impressed by women who can drink them under the table. You'll seem like a lush, and you'll probably do things that you'll regret the next day.

Likewise, men don't like women who swear like sailors and tell dirty jokes. It can be okay depending on the guy, once you know each other for a while, but swearing and dirty jokes don't create a good first impression.

PART III

Dating the Master Dater

When men play sports, they study the other team so they are familiar with its strengths and weaknesses. The same goes for dating. The more you know about men (the players), the better dater you will become.

This chapter will help you to understand how Master Daters play. Remember that you are the manager of your own social life. I will tell you which players to recruit and which ones you should trade, based on their stats (i.e., background, past experiences and current agenda).

Don't fret, honey. If you've done the preliminary work in the previous chapters, you are ready to play in the big leagues of dating.

A Man Will Treat a Woman the Way He Treats His Mother

One of the best ways to judge how a man is going to treat you after you're married is to observe how he treats his mother. If a man screams or hangs up on his mother, he'll probably do the same thing to you one day. This is why it's important to meet the mothers of the men you are seriously dating.

If he doesn't have a close relationship with his mom, you need to find out why. If he doesn't want you to meet his family, that's another red flag.

Years ago I had a personal trainer whom I considered dating. He was an excellent trainer, but I began to notice that he seemed bitter and angry when he talked about his female clients. So one day I asked him about his mother. It turned out his mom had left his father (and family) for another man. My trainer didn't trust women, and he probably never will.

Many of us grew up in dysfunctional families, which

Dating Training Film

***In The Company of Men* (1997),**
Neil LaBute, Writer and Director

Although there are countless films featuring misogynist characters (see the works of Jack Nicholson), this movie is the Mount Everest of women haters. The two leads are salesmen who are transferred to some godforsaken corporate park somewhere in middle America.

They spice up their otherwise mundane jobs by waging a bet about which one can coax a sweet young secretary, who also happens to be deaf, into falling in love with him. Afterward (just for the fun of it) they would break her heart by dumping her like yesterday's garbage.

If you haven't already encountered a woman hater, or you think you may be dating one, study this film carefully. It exposes the dark truth about how some sick men get their ya yas from mind-fucking innocent women. Thelma and Louise should have put a bullet through these guys.

doesn't mean that we can't work out our issues and live normal lives. But men who hate their mothers are often misogynists and, sadly for them, neither marriage nor dating material. (See "The Misogynist" on p. 1170.)

If a Man Is Mean to Service People, He'll Be Mean to You

If your date snaps his fingers at waiters or yells at his secretary, he'll probably treat you just as badly one day. If he's willing to stab an underling in the back in order to advance his career, watch your own back.

The way a man behaves with service people is a good

indication of how he operates in other areas of his life. Chances are, if he's gracious, honest and supportive to his staff, he'll be honest and supportive to you.

Never mistake those who need to put other people down in order to feel superior as being perfectionists or powerful. Honey, they are scum. In fact, the higher your status in life, be it in business or personal wealth, the more benevolent and courteous you should be to those who work for you.

If it turns you on to watch a man abusing his power, look within yourself for feelings of powerlessness. This kind of Machiavellian behavior shows that he is overcompensating for feelings of weakness.

Men Fantasize About Sex, Not Relationships

I had a friend in college who was stunningly beautiful. She had lots of boyfriends, but she would always talk about how she would end up marrying a professional athlete. When I met her years later, she was stuck on a basketball player whom she had dated casually.

She was sending him gifts, showing up at his hotel, and going to all of his games whenever he was in town. Even when he got engaged to another woman, she refused to believe that he didn't love her. She never thought of herself as a groupie, and she was convinced that her affection for him was requited. The truth was, she was just another port of call. She discovered this the hard way when she went up to him after a game and he didn't know who she was.

Men fantasize about sex; women fantasize about relationships. It starts when we are teenagers and we practice writing our boyfriend's last name, or dream about some movie star who will pick us out of the crowd and marry us. Most of us grow out of these childhood fantasies, but some do not.

Ask yourself the following:

1. Are you apart from your beau more than you are together?
2. Do you find yourself daydreaming about your love every chance you get?
3. Has he ever told you he loves you?
4. Does he call you almost every day?
5. Have you ever introduced this guy to your family or friends?
6. Is he married or engaged?
7. Has he ever been to your apartment or home?
8. Does he avoid seeing you in public?
9. Would you describe your relationship as primarily sexual?

If you answered yes to 1, 2, 6, 8, 9 and no to 3, 4, 5, wake up, Sleeping Beauty, you're living in a dream! You are not in a real relationship, so check your fantasy at the door.

Monica Lewinsky is a famous example of a woman whose relationship was pure fantasy. To this day, she believes that the President of the United States actually *loved* her and was not using her for sex. Girl, if you feel this way about a guy, get yourself some help. You clearly feel that you don't deserve anything better than a phantom boyfriend.

A Man Who Cheats on His Wife or Girlfriend Will Cheat on You

Honey, your great-great-grandmother could have told you this. Dating with integrity means never stealing another woman's husband or boyfriend. If you decide to sleep with a married man, don't even start with that woe-is-mistress-me. If more women dated with integrity, we wouldn't have so many broken marriages and broken hearts.

Dating Training Film

***Fatal Attraction* (1987), Adrian Lyne, Director**

This movie has become a buzz word for obsessed single women, and it scared the shit out of cheating men everywhere. It also gave us one of the most memorable screen characters in the form of a female stalker.

Glenn Close plays a high-powered businesswoman who falls head over pumps in love with Michael Douglas. Douglas has the great job, the trophy wife, the cute kid and the house in the 'burbs. His oh-so-perfect world disintegrates quickly when Close wants to play a central role in his life.

Women in the audience silently cheer her on when she screams "I will not be ignored!" but society must punish the sexually voracious career woman. Like the man-eating *Jaws* of the dating world, Close becomes a bunny-roasting monster, and the audience (especially the men) demand that the bitch must die!

I once dated a professional athlete I met at a party. He was dancing with a famous singer, so I kept looking over at them. He must have noticed my glances, because he motioned to me to come over and dance with them. I ignored him, thinking that he was motioning to someone else. *You*, he mouthed, pointing in my direction, *come dance with us!*

When I didn't budge from my seat, he got off the dance floor and said, "Oh, you're a lady. I have to personally ask you to dance, don't I?"

"That's right," I told him. "But I also need to know if it's all right with your girlfriend."

"She's not my girlfriend," he explained. "She's just a friend of mine."

So I danced with him, and we eventually started dating. But not until I was absolutely certain that he was single and available. This is what I call dating with integrity.

If a man tells you he's unhappily married and wants to date you, tell him, "Sure, as soon as you're divorced." If you find yourself attracted to a married man, become friends with his wife. Not so you can steal him away, but so you can discover what kind of woman attracted the type the man you want.

I learned this trick from the wife of a co-worker who was interested in me. Her husband would go home and talk about me all the time. One day she came to work and invited me out to lunch. Just the two of us. She wanted to find out what qualities I had that turned her husband's head.

She was so nice and gracious that we became friends. Even if I *wanted* to sleep with her husband, I wouldn't dream of betraying a friend. They're still married today.

I realize, of course, that no matter how much I rail against dating married men, single women will continue to reach for the golden ring. In Europe and other continents, men who have a wife, family and mistress are considered to have their basic needs met.

If you're currently dating a married man, tell him to come clean to his wife or you'll do it for him. At least you'll know where you stand.

If the relationship was meant to be, he will leave his wife for you. Publisher Harold Evans left his first wife for *Talk* editor Tina Brown. Paul Newman left his first wife for Joanne Woodward. These couples seem completely in love and compatible.

But more often than not, guys will keep coming up with excuses about why they can't leave. ("My wife needs me right now." I want to wait until the kids are older.") And why the hell *should* he leave when he's got it going on both sides?

Men Know How to Disappear

Consider it a gift if a guy pulls a disappearing act early in the dating process. It doesn't mean there's something wrong with you! He's just scared. Or maybe he's dating other women.

A guy who disappears for days or weeks at a time without word one, then suddenly calls you when he's ready to hook up again, doesn't want or respect you. Honey, he's not just disappearing on you, he's dissing you.

Let him go, and for heaven's sake, don't call him. Have some pride. Chasing after a man will just make him run faster. Why would you want to be with someone who doesn't want to be with you?

If he calls you after a few weeks of silence with some lame excuse, act as though you hardly noticed he was gone. Tell him about all the wonderful things you've been up to, and ask him, cheerfully, how he's been. If you decide you want to see him again, don't make a date with him immediately. Tell him you'll be busy for a while, but he can call you in the next few weeks. You don't have to give up on him entirely if you don't want to, but understand that this relationship will remain casual.

This is not game-playing as much as it is simple dating etiquette. Men who disappear are sending a message that they need time by themselves, or with other women. That's fine. But he can't expect you to sit around waiting for Mr. Thang to give you a jingle.

If a Man Says He's Never Been in Love, He Isn't Capable of Loving You

If a man tells you he's never been in love with anyone before, it's a good bet that he does not, and will not, love you either.

I'm suspicious of men over thirty who say they've never been in love. He might be able to *like* you, but *love* you? Think again, girlfriend.

These men do not allow themselves to trust anyone or to be vulnerable. What this really means is that he does not love himself. I know it's a cliché, but you have to love yourself before you can love anyone else.

Emotionally healthy people fall in love at some point in their lives, even if it isn't reciprocated, and even if it is simply a crush. Falling in love is a part of natural human development. Beware of this loveless lad, because he has set up a wall around his emotions that you will never be able to penetrate.

Falling in love means allowing yourself to be hurt; perhaps he was hurt so badly by someone in the past that he thinks it's better not to feel at all than to feel pain. This is no way to live, and he's certainly no one to love.

When a Man Says, "You're Not My Type," Believe Him

If you're lucky enough to date a man who is being honest with you, the least you can do in return is believe him. When he says, "You're not my type," no amount of plastic surgery or therapy is going to change that fact. The more important question should be, Is he *your* type?

The answer, no matter what you may think at the time, is no, because your "type" is someone who is madly, passionately in love with you as you are right now.

Men are unapologetic about their personal tastes when it comes to women. If you were a fly on the wall of a men's locker room, you'd know exactly what I'm talking about. "I want my woman to have more than a handful." Or, "She needs to be an old-fashioned kind of girl."

It may not be politically correct to have these particular requirements, but how fair is it to only date men who are over six feet or have more than a handful of hair? There's nothing wrong with having these provisos.

However, if you find a man who meets your other requirements, but happens to be 5'9", you might want to give him a chance anyway. You might discover that those few inches don't matter as much to you as you thought they did. If height is that important to you, it's better to know that now than after you're married and cheating with the local basketball team.

I've coached women who tell me, "I'd never date a Southern man." I ask them, "Have you ever tried?" Other women won't date any man who isn't a professional. My advice to these women is to remember that your goal is to DATE, not marry. One of my clients who said she didn't like New Age men ended up marrying an acupuncturist.

You never know if you don't try. In fact, men who you think are incompatible, for whatever reason, can be wonderful auditions for the real thing. You'll be more relaxed on the date because you won't be trying so hard to impress him. If you don't practice, and make your mistakes, you won't be ready when the right man comes along. It's like being in the batting cage. You swing, you miss, you swing again, and you hit a home run.

When a Man Says, "I'm Not Good Enough for You," Believe Him

When I was in high school, boys used to tell me, "You're too good for me." I'd tell them, "That's not true, you're a nice guy." I refused to believe them, and I ended up getting hurt.

If you choose not to believe a man who tells you he's no good, he'll prove it to you in some other way. He'll end up doing something terrible so you will eventually leave him. Men get uncomfortable when you don't allow their true nature to come out. And if you call them on their behavior, they'll say, "Baby, I told you that I was a snake." And they'd be right.

Men Who Need to Find Themselves Aren't Looking for Marriage

Any man, whatever his age, who tells you he is still trying to "find" himself is not looking for marriage or even a serious relationship. If he tells you this, get out before you get hurt. Men work on their careers first, and settle later. They know that relationships take a lot of work, and they can only concentrate on one thing at a time.

A man who is developing himself doesn't have the time to devote to the relationship. And once he's achieved his goal, he's usually a different kind of person with different needs. He will probably be attracted to someone who sees him *after* he's successful, not before. At this point he believes that he can do better than you, the one who accepted him without all the trappings of success. Not fair, not kind, but true.

Take the actor/comedian Jim Carrey. He struggled for years trying to eek out a living as a stand-up comic. His wife, with whom he has a child, stuck by him through all the hard times. As soon as he started getting some recognition, as soon as the money starting rolling in by the truckload, he dumped her for one of his beautiful co-stars. Not fair, not kind, but true.

This is why you must develop yourself before, during and after you get involved in a relationship. Never put your life on hold so a man can pursue his dreams. Have some dreams of your own.

More Ugly Truths About Men

Okay, men sometimes do behave badly. It's just a fact of life. It's your job to separate the men from the boys, and have a fine-tuned radar. Here are a few common manly misdeeds:

- **Men use women for sex.** This is why I tell you to hold out for as long as you can. By answering the booty call, you are his sleeping partner, not his date. Don't be so eager to give him sex. I don't care how much he bitches and moans, he'll respect you.
- **Men cheat on women they love.** This is sad but true. When a man cheats on a woman he loves, and who loves him, he is saying he doesn't deserve to be loved. Men who suffer from self-esteem issues will almost always put themselves in a situation where they test a woman to see if she really, truly loves him. Bill Clinton is an excellent example of this. I believe Clinton really loves Hillary, but he doesn't feel he is good enough for her.

  One reason women find married men so attractive is because we see only the fantasy, not the day-to-day take-out-the-garbage reality. The latter, of course, is the side that his wife gets to see.

  Likewise, he sees you only at your best, in your fine lingerie, going out for romantic dinners, hiding your affair from others (another turn-on) and leaving before you open your mascara-smudged eyes in the morning.

  When it comes to chronic cheaters, I say three strikes and they're out. After the third time, there are no more excuses. The only way to deal with a cheater is to let him go. Tell him to give you a call when he's ready to be loved by one woman. You.
- **Some men shouldn't be married**. There are some men who treasure their freedom more than they will ever treasure a wife. These are the men who should stay bachelors. Trying to tie down this kind of man is a recipe for heartache, because they'll always have their eye on the exit. These are the men you have steamy, screamy affairs with and move on. You'll always have the memories.

Dating Training Film

***She's the One* (1996), Edward Burns, Director**

This is a romantic comedy about two brothers and the women who come between them. The film will teach you about men's moral ambiguity when it comes to sex and marriage.

While you're shaking your head saying, "How could he do that?" the man sitting next to you will be nodding his head knowingly. Don't shield yourself from the truth, girlfriends. The more you know, the better equipped you will be to deal with the real world of dating and relationships.

Men Know It's Okay to Look But Not Touch

Life would be so much easier if women understood this simple truth. Just because a man looks at another woman doesn't mean he wants to sleep with her. Sure, he might fantasize about making love to her, but he won't (for the most part) act on it.

Don't be threatened when your date looks at another women. Men are visual. They are basically the same sexually as they were when they were fourteen years old, only now they don't have to hide the *Playboy*s under the pillow. My boyfriend's first sexual experience was seeing Sophia Loren in black lingerie. From that day on, he always gets excited when he sees a woman in a black teddy.

Likewise, you should be free to revel in the beauty of the male form. Let him know that seeing Mark Wahlberg in his skivvies makes you weak in the knees. Visual appreciation is a two-way street. Believe me, men understand this concept. If he's secure in his own sexuality, he'll be able to say, "Yeah, he's a good-looking guy."

If it makes him uncomfortable to hear you complimenting other men's physical attributes, keep your lascivious thoughts to yourself. The exception to this rule is if he openly ogles beautiful women. In that case, there are no foul flags. You've had to look at billboard-sized breasts your whole life! Thank you, Mr. Calvin Klein, for the equal opportunity.

Men Need to Bond with Their Buddies

One of the fastest ways to get rid of a man is to come between him and his pals. Men bond with their friends differently than they do with women. In many ways, they are much more loyal to each other than women are. Women who are desperate to be with a man will drop a girlfriend in a red-hot minute if he doesn't like her.

Honey, boyfriends come and go, but a strong friendship can last forever if you nurture it. Men understand this about friendship, so it's not your place to call his buddy a loser, even if you think he is one. Attacking his pal will make him want to defend him even more. If you really can't stand his best bud, give him a weekly boys' night out and stay at home with a good video or with one of your own girlfriends.

Conversely, if the guy you're dating doesn't like one of your friends, sit down with him and find out why. Tell him that she's been in your life longer than he has, and she's been supportive of you in a way that only a girlfriend can be.

See if you can't get him to appreciate what it is you value in her. If this doesn't work, let it go. Accept that your friend and boyfriend will always be like oil and water, and see her when he's hanging with his boys.

Men Like to Fix Things

Women need to learn that our mate is not our girlfriend. He may not listen to you the way your friends do when you have a problem. He's more action-oriented. He'll want to fix the problem. If you want somcone to listen to you, talk to your girlfriend. If you want someone to solve your problem, talk to your mate.

Asking a man to fix something for you will make him feel like a hero. Men love to feel needed.

Men Like to Be Rescuers

When I say men like to be rescuers, I don't mean you should hang by your fingernails from a bridge. I'm not talking about big crises here. But you can let them rescue you in small ways.

Most women are afraid of bugs. If you have an eight-legged creature in your house, why not call him and ask him to help you get rid of it. I once knew a woman who was afraid of mice (how cliché!). When she saw one scampering across her floor, she called a male friend who lived around the corner to put it outdoors. She was so scared after that that he spent the night on the couch and subsequently their relationship evolved to an entirely new level.

If your car is on the blink, for example, ask a man if he would mind taking a look under your hood before you take it to the mechanic. If you're thinking of buying a new computer, men love to give advice about what kind you should get. He might even go comparison shopping with you. (Computer and car shopping are two of the few kinds of shopping men volunteer for.)

If he can program a VCR, fix your computer, build a kitchen shelf or simply make you feel safer, let him know how much you cherish his help.

I was in the park with one of my clients recently when she saw a cute guy she wanted to meet. She quickly strapped on her Rollerblades, skated over and fell right down in front of him. As he gallantly helped her up, she apologized, saying, "I'm so sorry, I haven't learned how to stop yet." He gave her a skating lesson right then and there. When I ran over to see if she was okay, she winked at me. I was so proud!

Another tip that I teach my clients is to act like a tourist in your own hometown or city. Stand a foot away from a landmark and say, "Excuse me, sir. Do you know where I can find Bloomingdale's?" I guarantee you, most men are eager to give directions, even if they won't take them. He'll probably say, "Where are you going?" or "Are you from around here?" Nine times out of ten he'll walk you right to where you want to go.

When you tell a man, "What would I have done without you?" what you're really doing is verbally polishing his armor.

By the Time a Man Says He Loves You, He Probably Does

We all know that men treat the L-word as if it's some infectious disease. They would rather be intimate than talk about it. It's almost a cliché, but even the most evolved men have trouble talking about their feelings or saying "I love you" to anything but their family pets.

The key for women is not to focus so much on what a man says, but to observe what a man *does*. Women have to do away with their romantic ideals. I know it's hard to change a lifetime of programming, but I promise you'll be much happier if you start thinking more like a man (or, at least, understand the way men think).

The following are examples of the different ways that men and women express their love and affection:

	Women	Men
I.	Buying flowers and jewelry	Buying lingerie
II.	Writing love notes	Calling once a day
III.	Planning a date	Showing up
IV.	Planning a vacation	Sex in a hotel
V.	Renting *The Way We Were*	Renting *Debbie Does Dallas*
VI.	Going to a wedding together	Wearing a tux
VII.	Defending your honor	Beating the bastard up
VIII.	Taking you out to dinner	Taking out the garbage

Men and women have different ideas about what constitutes a romantic gesture. If a man is fixing up your house or helping you buy a new car, he's showing you by his actions that he loves you. It's the little things that he does for you that tell you how he feels.

My brother Tim rarely says the "L" word, but whenever he comes over to visit, he'll check to see if I have enough to eat. When faced with an empty fridge, he'll say, "You need groceries. Can I go out and get you some milk?" This is the way he *shows* me that he loves me.

In contrast, a woman will tell a man that she's falling in love after three dates. Wrong, wrong, wrong. Nothing will put the kibosh on a relationship faster than a premature profession of love.

Ken, a thirty-year-old bachelor and computer programmer from New York, was looking forward to dating Meg, an attractive woman whom he had met at a bar the previous weekend. She had told him that she was planning to move to California in a month, so he thought they could both relax and have some casual fun.

On the second date, however, Meg told Ken that she was

thinking of staying in New York because of him. Ken didn't know how she could have misinterpreted his eagerness to date as a signal to dock her boat in his port.

Girlfriend, it takes a long time to love a person. You can love a piece of chocolate after one bite, but you can't love a man after dating him for a few weeks. Men like to invest time in a woman before they tell her they love her. To them, women are like stocks that are watched and nurtured to see if the emotional index goes up or down.

If you start to free-fall and you need to say something about it, tell him you're falling in "like." Don't jump the gun on the love connection, because you are showing your cards too soon. Let him wonder how you feel. Plus, what you may think is love may actually be lust or, more likely in a woman's case, your desire to be in love.

Men Borrow Money from Banks, Not Girlfriends

Don't lend money to a man, even if he promises to pay you back immediately, because you'll end up resenting him for it. Financial obligations can ruin the best of relationships. If a guy asks to borrow money from you, tell him you can't afford it, even if you can. You are not the Bank of America.

Borrowing money from women can be a scam for some men, who use their charms and a woman's need to be in a relationship as bait. Suggest that he go to a friend or relative, or that he find a job to get him over the financial hump. If he balks, pleads or calls you a cheapskate, drop the deadbeat.

Likewise, don't borrow money from your date, because it tips the power balance too much in his direction. Money issues destroy more relationships than any other single issue.

Ten Signs That He's Interested

1. He calls all the time.
2. He acts jittery when he's around you.
3. He introduces you to his family and business associates.
4. He wants to spend the holidays with you.
5. He sends you cards and flowers.
6. He plays with your child or pet.
7. He wants to go away for the weekend.
8. He asks you questions about your future goals.
9. He asks you out a week in advance.
10. He charms your parents.

Men Know That Excuses Don't Fly

If a man doesn't produce up to the level that is expected of him at work, he's going to get put on probation or fired. Why should it be different in the dating world?

Women should not accept lame excuses from men who are undependable. The only difference is, if your date or boyfriend behaves irresponsibly, instead of writing him up, you should write him off.

If you find yourself with a man who is constantly coming up with reasons for his unreliable behavior, start waving a big red flag. A real man pays his own bills, pays his alimony and child support on time and gets up and goes to work in the morning.

It's wonderful to be an actor, artist or writer, but you need a man who brings home a paycheck in order for the relationship to survive. Everyone goes through hard times, so if a man is unemployed or underemployed, he should be either looking for work, or doing some other kind of work that pays him until he finds the job in his chosen field.

I have a neighbor who is a successful businesswoman in her early forties. She's divorced and currently dating an unemployed actor. She's been frustrated by always being the one to pay for dinner and a movie whenever they go out, but she doesn't want to rock the boat by telling her boyfriend that she is annoyed with her role as sugar mama. She's afraid that she'll never find anyone better, and she doesn't want to give up the sex. This is a relationship based on fear, not love.

The bottom line is this: If the hard times drag on for longer than six months, you may have to stop seeing him until he gets a job. Unless he is physically ill, he should be gainfully employed.

Unless you're married, never support a man who is unemployed but could be working, even if he promises to pay you back as soon as he gets a job. I can't tell you how many stories I've heard about women who have dipped into their savings to support their boyfriends, only to be dumped and chumped out of their money after the relationship ended.

If you must play the role of Ms. Dole, get a written agreement from your boyfriend about how and when he will reimburse you. This way you have some legal protection should he try to skip out on you and his debt.

Men who make excuses for their inability to find a job are either lying or in denial. Excuses mean "I don't want to." Excuses mean "I don't have to." Excuses mean "I don't care." Don't be fooled by excuses, and never support a man who refuses to look for work.

Men Like to Have Their Egos Stroked

Men are simple creatures. Sure, they like sex, but if you stroke a man's ego, you will have him eating out of your manicured little hands.

Now, I'm not saying you should laugh at his jokes if they're not funny, or pretend he's Bill Gates when he starts talking about Macs versus PCs. Men may not be able to tell when a woman fakes an orgasm, but unless he's dumb and dumber's second cousin, a man can tell when you're faking a conversation. Be truthful and be yourself.

The time to pump a man up is when he does something wonderful. A man will respect you more if you tell him straight out that his joke wasn't funny. Tease him about it: "That joke isn't funny, but the other story you told was a riot."

One of the best ways to pump a man up is to say nice things about him to his family and friends. I was at a dinner once with a couple who had been married for twenty-five years. When she got up from the table, her husband turned to me and said, "Isn't she the best?"

We have a tendency to break each other down when we go through hard times, and we sometimes talk about our partner's faults to others in the hope that they'll take our side. Keep those negative things to yourself when you're in public.

Let him know, as well, that he makes you happy. Tell him what it is that you love about him. A man wants a woman who believes in her heart of hearts that he is wonderful. He wants to be that knight in shining armor that we dream about. He needs to know that when he's with you, he is your hero.

Men like compliments, but praise can be a double-edged sword. If it comes naturally to you, like it does to me, paying someone a compliment is a gift that you give to others. If they're phony, compliments fall flat.

There is always something in a man that's special, whether it's his brains or his biceps. You will make his day by acknowledging what is special about him. If you have trouble complimenting others, think of it as an acknowledgment instead.

Truthfully, women have a harder time accepting compliments than men do. Women have been brainwashed into thinking that accepting a compliment means they're egotistical. They need to get to the point where they can take it in, accept it and say thank you. If you contradict someone who says, "You look great in that dress," by saying, "You think so? I feel fat in this dress," what you're really saying is that you don't like yourself very much.

If a man is overcomplimenting you, touch his hand gently and say, "Thank you, I appreciate that, but you're beginning to embarrass me." Men will do that when they're feeling overwhelmed by you. Letting him know that you are just a regular person will put him at ease. If a man feels safe with you, he'll relax and start being himself.

Clues That a Man Isn't Interested in You

- **He doesn't call you.** (Hello!)
- **His eyes are darting around the room while you're together.** (He's checking out the other women in the room.)
- **He makes calls on his cell phone.** I don't care how important he thinks he is, unless he's a doctor, he should leave the damn cell phone or beeper home when you're on a date.
- **He shows no interest in what you're saying.** If he continues to change the subject or glaze over when you talk, he's in his own world, and there's no room in it for you.
- **He says things that are blatantly offensive, sarcastic, suggestive or downright mean.** This is a technique that some men use to sabotage a date so you'll hate him and never want to see him again. He may start to make off-color remarks or tell offensive stories. Just tell him

Why Men Don't Always Mean It When They Say, "I'll Call You"

Let's face it, girlfriend, men will sometimes promise to call you when they have absolutely no intention of doing so. This is just part of the phone numbers game. Here are some of the reasons why a man won't call:

- **You're dripping with jewelry, and he's a jeans and T-shirt kind of guy.** If he sees you in your jewels and finery, he may think you are out of his league. You may be a jeans and T-shirt kind of woman on the weekends, but he doesn't know that. Don't overdo the jewelry on your first date. In this case, less is more. Most men don't know squat about jewelry, and all they can think about when they see gems is your jones for a diamond.

  This is why you have to match your wardrobe with the man you're dating. Men are visual. Women are emotional. You may feel an emotional connection with him, while he's thinking, "I'll never be able to afford to buy her jewelry like that."
- **You are too businesslike.** This is especially a problem in the big cities. If you are taking calls on your cell phone every three minutes, the man might think you care about business more than you care about him. Men love women who are powerful in their jobs, but leave your cell phone at home. It's okay to work hard, as long as you play hard as well.
- **He has another girlfriend.** Men date like men, which means they may have a few other women on the side. If he doesn't call you, he may be calling someone else in his little black PowerBook.
- **You didn't meet his checklist requirements.** Dating is mutual interviewing, so while you're seeing if he fits your list of requirements, he's checking off his own list. Some men are

you'd rather not talk about these things, and if he persists, leave. You should never sit through a date just to be polite if you are feeling uncomfortable or upset.

- **He won't stop talking about his old girlfriend.** Women do this, too. But if a man is telling you about his ex while you're out on a date, tell him politely that you'd rather not talk about it. If he continues, make yourself an ex-date.

When a Man Says He's Not Ready to Commit, He's Not Ready to Commit to You

Men have a problem with monogamy today because so many women have made it easy for them not to. This is why I'm an advocate of waiting until you have an engagement ring before moving in together. Once again, our grandmothers were right when they told us, "Why buy the cow when you can get the milk for free?"

The truth is, unless a man is a perpetual bachelor, he will probably commit when he is good and ready. It just may not be with you. Women who believe cohabitation is a dress rehearsal for marriage are sadly mistaken, because men have no trouble packing up their boxes and moving into another woman's place. They are not nesters by nature, so they don't form attachments to their homes the way women do.

A dresser is a dresser is a dresser. As long as there's a working fridge, hot shower and couch, a man will feel right at home.

I have a friend who lived with a man for years hoping that they would eventually marry. She kept giving him ultimatums, and he kept ignoring them. After seven years she finally made good on her threats, and kicked him out. Three months later, he was married to another woman.

When a man is ready, he is ready, and he will marry the first woman he falls in love with. My friend's biggest mistake was closing herself off for seven years to other men who might have been better for her. Don't waste your time with men who don't want to commit.

The Players

Master Daters know how to avoid certain types of women when they date. They know who the real contenders are, and who doesn't stand a chance. They recognize the warning signs early in the game, and they make their decisions about whether or not to stay or run away pretty quickly. Nothing wrong with that; dating is the process of separating the wheat from the chaff.

Women must start applying the same *caveat emptor* (buyer beware) attitude when dating. Here are common types of men that are about as much fun as a tax audit whom you should avoid at all costs.

THE UNEMPLOYED MAN

It's great to be an actor, artist or writer, but you need a man who brings home a paycheck in order for the relationship to survive. Everyone goes through hard times, so he should be either looking for work, or doing some other kind of work that pays.

If you're dating an under- or unemployed man, you can still do fun things together like rent movies, go to museums and free concerts, take long walks and bike rides or pack a picnic lunch. But if the hard times drag on for longer than six months, you may have to stop seeing him until he gets a job. Some men can become awfully comfortable with a sugar mama on their arms.

THE MISOGYNIST

Men who hate women still pursue them, because it's their mission in life to make women miserable. Misogynists have been hurt badly by the opposite sex (possibly starting with their own mothers) and, therefore, unconsciously believe that all women are bitches.

Dating Training Film

***About Last Night*, (1986) Edward Zwick, Director**

This movie is riddled with mistakes that women make. Remember when Rob Lowe and Demi Moore first meet at the bar in Chicago? He's eyeing her from across the room and she's eyeballing him right back. He interprets her attention as an invitation to come over and talk to her. His line is a perfectly good one: "I couldn't help notice you noticing me." Her response: "I wasn't looking at you, I was looking at the clock above your head."

Now, if a man is brave enough to make the first move, be gracious. He's not going to like you more because you came up with a witty line. In fact, he's going to think you're a bitch. Remember that your purpose in being there is to meet men, not knock them down.

Understand that men are basically insecure. They're afraid of being rejected. Most men, unless they're players, don't think, "I'm going to bag this babe." When guys walk up to you for the first time, they're thinking, "I hope she won't humiliate me."

When you first meet someone, why not give him the benefit of the doubt? Why not decide to like the person, in spite of what anyone else may have said, until he gives you a reason not to? Sure, there are mean, selfish, unpleasant people in this world. But prejudging people only closes you off further and decreases the number of datable men. Baby, you want to increase your circle of friends, not shrink it!

These men usually reject any and all glances from the well-intentioned woman. They might even ignore your attempts to start up a conversation. These are the harmless ones. The dangerous misogynists will try to attract you, gain your trust, then verbally or physically abuse you.

It doesn't matter how nice or beautiful you are, he will hate you no matter what you do. You're female, therefore you are the enemy. In fact, he'll probably hate you more because you're nice or beautiful.

Don't get sucked in by a misogynist's charm. The first time he ignores you, disses you or, God forbid, lays a hand on you, run for your life! In the same way that the misogynist's past has taught him how to abuse women, women who are attracted to misogynists are repeating patterns that they learned as little girls.

It goes something like this: If your father abused your mother, chances are you will be attracted to a woman-hater because that's the only way you know how to get attention from men. If you're seeing a shrink, you know this already. If you're not and you're attracted to these types of men, you probably should be.

Whatever the reasons, girlfriend, don't ever accept abuse from any man! And don't try to get even with him by putting him down. If he sees that he's gotten you angry or upset, he has already won. This is part of his sick little game. The best thing you can do is to walk away. It makes him happy to see women suffer.

Remember, there are plenty of men out there who love women, and who want to make you happy.

THE TEASE

Women aren't the only ones who use their bodies to tease the opposite sex. The Tease has been handsome all his life, so he's used to being surrounded by admirers. There's no challenge in getting a woman into bed, that's easy.

The Tease wears clothes that accentuate his body. The message he sends is, "You can look but you can't touch." The minute you try to approach him, he heads for the exit.

He's usually a good dancer, so you'll see him shaking his booty back and forth like a flag in the wind. Some women are fooled into thinking that this mating dance is a sexual overture. But as soon as the song is over, he'll disappear into the crowd. Before you know it he's back on the dance floor with another woman, shaking his groove thing in her face. The Teaser gets off on turning on as many women as possible, but he's a hit-and-run driver.

THE BARFLY

This is a man who uses women to support his drinking habit. If you're in your right mind, you will see that his love of libations is more than social drinking. If you don't, you are in danger of being sucked into his vortex of alcoholism.

Feeling sorry for him or trying to help him in the usual female way will only push him farther down the road of self-destruction. If your dates begin and end with a cocktail, give him the number to AA and toast to his sobriety.

THE HOMEBOY

This type of man likes to travel in packs. Without his homies, he is the lone wolf with no one to support him or egg him on to approach us chickens. The homeboys may be single, married or a combination of both.

They come to the club or bar to have a few drinks and shoot the bull—with each other. Some just want to socialize among themselves, just like we do with our girlfriends; they don't want to be bothered by single women giving them the eye. They are afraid that if you reject them, they will lose face with their posse.

If you see a man you are interested in hanging with his boys, don't try to break into the huddle. They are either planning their next move, or talking about their wives and girlfriends.

If a lone wolf happens to break away from the pack in order to give you his phone number, make sure you meet him again without his buds. This way you'll get to know if there's a man inside that posturing boy.

THE RINGMASTER

Married men also go out in groups, but they're usually slumped over their drinks looking like their dog just died. In the old days, they took off their rings. Nowadays, they consider themselves girl magnets. They like the thrill of bungee-jumping into the single world again.

If a married man approaches you, don't give him your pity. Honey, you don't have time to listen to his woe-is-married-me stories. If he is in so much pain, tell him to get counseling or to go home and have this conversation with his wife.

THE FORTUNE HUNTER

This is the man whose main interest is the interest you're earning in your bank account. You can spot the Fortune Hunter (also known as the gigolo) by the kinds of questions he asks: "What do you do for a living?" "How much money do you make?" What kind of car do you drive?" "What did your house or apartment cost?"

He knows all the designer names, and he'll check your labels and watch when you're not looking. He flits from wealthy woman to wealthy woman like a socialite butterfly, leaving as soon as he has sufficiently drained them of their savings, money markets and 401ks.

If you are a woman of means, make sure that money does not become a topic of conversation on your dates. No one needs to know about your portfolio until you're ready to walk down the aisle. (And if he asks you to marry him after the third date, he's thinking alimony, not matrimony.)

Fortune Hunters are often drop-dead good-looking. If you're not, chances are he's not entranced by your great personality. Fortune Hunters prey on older, plain and desperately lonely women.

Honey, I don't care how old, ugly or desperate you are, being alone and wealthy is better than being in a loveless relationship and broke.

THE LADIES' MAN

Ladies' Men make good boyfriends, but bad husbands. Handsome and charming won't help you when you're in your tenth hour of labor screaming for a hand to hold.

If you're dating a Ladies' Man, ask yourself if he's the kind of person you would want your son to grow up to be. Will he be there for you when you get sick? The answer will tell you whether this man is either affair or handle-with-care material. When you're with a Ladies' Man, he will make you feel as though there's no one in the world but you. He *genuinely* likes women.

I know, because my father is a Ladies' Man. He's 6'5" and knock-you-sideways gorgeous. He used to pitch for the New York Giants. He's seventy years old now and married to his seventh wife. My mother met him when she was twenty-nine. What my mother discovered too late was that my dad is the type of man you date, not marry.

You can learn a lot about yourself from a Ladies' Man. He will hold up a mirror to you and show you how wonderful you are when you can't do that for yourself. He will help build your confidence, which you can take with you for the rest of your life.

In fact, they tend to go after women who have low self-esteem. They will tell a beautiful woman she's smart and tell

Dating Training Films

The Works of Richard Gere

***American Gigolo* (1980), Paul Schrader, Director**

Nearly all of Richard Gere's work is dating training films, starting with *American Gigolo*, his first major role. Here he plays a male prostitute who is left without an alibi after his ex-client is murdered. As in most Hollywood films featuring prostitutes, he falls in love with one of his beautiful Janes (Lauren Hutton).

This film is more about Gere's gorgeous young body than anything else. It features full-frontal nudity (his) and a declaration by Gere's character, Julian, that it took him three hours to get one older woman to climax. Bravo! It's a tough job, but someone's got to do it.

Watch this film for the pure fantasy of having a man whose single goal for the evening is to please you, even if you he had to use your American Express card to do it.

***An Officer and a Gentleman* (1982), Taylor Hackford, Director**

The ultimate rescue film that ends with officer recruit (Richard Gere) literally sweeping beleaguered factory worker (Debra Winger) off her feet. As in most of Gere's relationship films, there is an insidious message within this plotline. Although you want to let men rescue

a smart woman that she's beautiful. If you meet a Ladies' Man, date him, have fun with him, bask in his charm, but don't, under any circumstances, marry him!

THE ONE-NIGHT STAND

These men buy condoms at bulk rate, if they use them at all. They need sex constantly, and for them variety is the spice of their sex life. If you're looking to have your needs you in little ways (like fixing your VCR or broken cabinet), women should not depend on men to change their lives completely.

Women must come into relationships as whole people; our basic needs (food, shelter, work etc.) must already be met. Baby, do not wait for your prince (or, in this case, officer) to pluck you out of the muck that is your life. Sisters have to do that for themselves. Only then should you invite the gentleman along for the rest of the ride.

***Pretty Woman* (1990), Garry Marshall, Director**

In this Hollywood fantasy film, a high-powered M&A businessman (Richard Gere) hires a prostitute (Julia Roberts) to be his companion for a week. This Pygmalion story follows the couple as he tries to integrate the former streetwalker into high society.

Inevitably, the businessman and the audience fall in love with the ho, choosing to believe that (a) streetwalkers are beautiful, healthy and drug-free; (b) prostitutes actually enjoy having sex with men; and (c) all a bad girl needs is a good man to rescue her.

Girlfriend, this is not real life! Watch this film for the not-so-subtle Cinderella fairy tale that is at the root of so many of our fantasies about men and relationships.

satisfied for just one evening, go for it, girl, but safeguard your body and your emotions.

You won't have to make him breakfast in the morning, because he'll probably be gone by the time you open your eyes.

THE TRUMP

The Trump may be handsome, or he may just *think* he's handsome. Reality has nothing to do with it. He is the kind of guy who will spin everything he does into a success story.

He might even name buildings after himself. He is never wrong, and any problem he encounters is always the other person's fault.

You can spot him catching a glimpse of his own sweet self in the salt shaker, the mirror on the restaurant wall or shop window. He will drop names of people he knows, even if Mike Ovitz is a friend of a friend of a friend's cousin. He is simply nauseating, but some women choose to believe his self-promotion.

THE POSTER BOY

The Poster Boy is a physical work of art. He has the six-pack stomach, chiseled face and klieg-light smile. He looks like he just jumped off a billboard. He's easy on the eyes but empty between the ears.

When it comes to Poster Boys, I say, date away! Men have been going after eye candy and trophy girlfriends for centuries. If you're a powerful exec who wants a handsome date for a business function or wedding, call the Poster Boy.

So what if you're smarter than he is? He won't know the difference. You're only making small talk, anyway. You'll impress your friends and look good in the company news-letter photos. Cher had her bagel boy, you can have your Poster Boy.

THE ALPHA MAN

The Alpha Man is easy to spot because his surplus of testosterone (or steroids) produces an oversized body and ego. He enjoys race cars, boxing, hunting and extreme sports, especially if there's a possibility that he or someone else might be killed while engaging in them.

He often gets into fights with other Alphas, and sometimes he even ends up in jail. Many women are attracted to the Alpha because he's a bad boy and allows us to act out our own aggressions without suffering the consequences. The problem is, he sometimes acts out on us, and that can be risky for our health and well-being.

Boys may be boys, but honey, you're a grown-up now. If you find yourself attracted to an Alpha, it means that you are probably a bad girl yourself. Women like Whitney Houston, who go for the Bobby Browns of this world, should let the bad girls inside them come out instead. Don't live your fantasies vicariously through these men, because bad boys are not marriage material.

Go out with your girlfriends instead. Raise some hell until you get it out of your system. Or act it out in your fantasies, but don't, under any circumstances, hook up with an Alpha for the long run.

THE DESIRABLES

Dating books and magazines often talk about the undesirable men, but few give credit to the guys we would like to spend our time and lives with. Here are some examples of the types of men you *should* be going after. Don't overlook them!

THE NICE GUY

The old saying "Nice guys always finish last" is based on truth when it comes to dating. Women like challenges as much as men do, which is why being too nice as a man is just as much of a turn-off as it is when a woman is too nice. Giving too much too soon is overwhelming no matter who's doing the giving.

That being said, you must remember that looking for a boyfriend and a husband are two very different things. If you're looking for a husband (and you shouldn't be doing this in the beginning of your dating career), you will have a different set of criteria than if you are simply looking for a date.

Men who are edgy can make excellent dates. They're fun loving, free-spirited and a little dangerous. They don't always make great husbands, however. If you're looking for the father of your children, being responsible, trustworthy and, yes, nice is a good thing. Charlie Sheen might be a good lover, but Tom Hanks is definitely the better father.

The Nice Guy is actively seeking a girlfriend or wife. He is straight, unattached and considerate of your needs. I know you think the Nice Guy might be boring, but this is one of the easiest kinds of man to fall in love with.

He is the one at the party, club, office or baseball game looking for the same thing you are. He's the one who asks for your phone number and calls you the next day. He's the one who's genuinely interested in you, and doesn't care that you aren't perfect and neither is he. The reason you didn't notice him, honey, is because you were too busy looking at the pecs on the Alpha Man.

The Nice Guy knows what he wants when he sees it, and

Dating Training Film

***Broadcast News* (1987), James Brooks, Director**

In this film about the behind-the-scenes world of a network newscast, Albert Brooks plays the smart, funny nerd who never gets the girl (Holly Hunter). We are painfully aware throughout the film that he's the one for Hunter, but her fear of intimacy and need for independence prevent her from taking the bait.

Study the way Brooks tries to let Hunter know he's interested in her as more than a colleague. Brooks is the typical Nice Guy who gets shafted for the cute blond. Hunter goes for the golden boy, but gives him up in the end, not for Albert, but for the soul-mate she hopes to meet in the future.

Why she couldn't just look in her own backyard is frustrating, but very real. Is there anyone in your life who plays this role?

he goes after it. He is willing to wait for what he wants, especially if he thinks he has found his treasure.

You are the bright, shiny convertible he's always dreamed about. Admire this man for having the courage to go after what he wants, and for God's sake, give him a chance!

THE JOCK

If you are the type of woman who likes to play sports as well as watch them, the Jock is for you. This able-bodied boy skis in the winter and plays softball in the summer, touch football in the fall and basketball all year round. He has never met a sport he didn't like.

Don't even try for the Jock if your idea of a great date is a concert, play or museum. You've got to like hot dogs, flat beer and tailgate parties, and you won't mind wearing a team jersey or baseball cap (backward or forward). You should also enjoy getting your hands and hair dirty sliding into first base.

The Jock has sexual stamina, God bless his athletic self, although he might also have a wandering eye and not care a whole heck of a lot about pleasing you in bed. Scoring is the ultimate goal, of course, for the single Jock, and he likes a screamer in bed and in the stands.

THE NERD

Nerds have made a comeback lately, thanks to Bill Gates and Internet stocks. They may be ugly, but they're steady and safe. Their pencils aren't the only things they get protectors for.

As a woman gets older, Nerds start looking better and better. By then we've been through the Alphas and Ladies' Men, and we're just plain tired. You want a man who will be there when you call him at the office, and who will go with you to flea markets because he's not busy watching the games on Sunday.

If you're lucky, the Nerd might also be funny, because he reads books that don't have color panels in them. He probably likes children, and he won't embarrass you at your office Christmas party. Aren't these enough reasons to love a Nerd?

You can meet a Nerd at any computer convention or Comp USA. Ask him to help you pick out a PC or Mac, or to explain which is a better buy. (Make sure you have lots of time, because his explanation could take hours.)

Don't bother going for a Nerd if sex is vitally important to you. He either has some kinky *Star Trek* fantasies, or he sticks with the missionary position because it's the morally correct thing to do.

PART IV

Having a Game Plan

Having a game plan when you're dating means always keeping your goals in mind. You've done the preparation, the inner work, and you understand a little better how men think. The next step is knowing how to get what you're looking for.

If you find yourself getting sidetracked from your goal, take a break, recover, and go back to where you left off. It may mean doing more of the inner work. That's fine. You cannot skip steps if you want to reach your goal.

The Sexual Waiting Game (Men Hate It, But You Gotta Do It)

Women should wait at least four months before they have sex with a man they're seriously dating. Unfortunately, when it comes to sex, you must date more like a woman than like a man. The reason for this is that after the fourth month, the masks come off and you have a better idea of who he is. Intimacy only comes with time and the sharing of ideas, thoughts and emotions.

A one-night stand is okay if you are playing it safe (using a condom with spermicide) and you don't care if you ever see the guy again. But if you truly want the relationship to go the distance, you must wait.

Having sex on the first date is the fastest way to end a relationship. I know we've been taught to follow the three-date-wait (i.e., sex is okay after the third date), but that doesn't lead to commitment, either. After the fourth month, start having a conversation about sex.

If your date is pushing you to be more intimate, tell him, "I'm looking forward to this as much as you are, but I want to be sure that we're both ready to take this relationship to the next level. I want to be sure that the feelings we have for each other are real."

I know it seems like an eternity, but if you're following my program, you're not dating one man exclusively. You should be seeing him once a week, which means you will have only been together twelve times. In the meantime, you can both prepare for the big day by getting tested for AIDS and other STDs.

Getting tested is vital at any age. If a man has been single for a long time, he's probably slept with a lot of different women, one of whom could have been a prostitute or IV drug user. Even more reason to wait for the test results. I don't care what your partner has told you or how upstanding he may look, you're not just sleeping with him, you're sleeping with everyone he's ever slept with before you.

If you absolutely can't wait for the test results (and you should both be tested twice to make absolutely sure of a negative result), use a condom. Don't wait for *him* to bring the subject up. It's your body and it will be your baby if you get pregnant and he hits the road.

The best time to discuss birth control is before all your clothes are off, and in a safe place, like in a restaurant. If a man doesn't want to talk about birth control, you'd better rethink having sex with him. You *must* have this conversation. Don't let a few minutes of awkwardness result in a lifetime of sorrow.

Why wait so long? Because men take a longer time than women do to connect emotionally. They know how to connect physically, of course, but once a man has made an emotional connection with you, it will be hard for him to let you go. If he's just having sex for the pleasure of it, there is no spiritual bond.

Until a man has gone out with you for at least four months, you are the woman he's seeing, not his girlfriend.

To him, you are free agents, members of a different baseball team that can be traded at any time.

Women, on the other hand, will start calling a guy her boyfriend after four dates, even if there is no implicit commitment.

Men are not impulse buyers when it comes to the big-ticket items. And to a man, a woman is the ultimate big-ticket item. If you make a man wait, he'll treasure you more because he has invested more time in you.

I had a boyfriend once who wouldn't let me touch his stereo. He saved up for this stereo for five years and when he finally bought it, he didn't want anyone else touching it. Honey, if a man can wait that long for a piece of electronic equipment, he can take some time before he touches your equipment.

Many women feel that sex validates them and makes them more of a woman. If a woman hasn't had sex for a while, she feels as though she has somehow lost her desirability. Women must learn that they are sexual beings even if they do not have a sex partner.

Although sex is a biological need, men and women can go months, years and even a lifetime without sex. If you haven't had it in a while and you need some sexual relief, try pleasuring yourself (see "How to Have Sex Like a Man" on p. 161). It may not be as romantic, but it gets the job done.

If you feel the need for someone to reach out and touch you, get a massage. Exercise to release some of that sexual tension. Hug a friend. Call an old lover. Go online and have cybersex. Watch a porn flick. Read an erotic novel. There are plenty of things you can do to maintain your sensuality.

Men believe that bad sex is better than no sex at all. But every woman who has had bad sex (which is almost every woman) knows that a pint of mint chocolate chip can be better than bad sex.

Men Know How to Advertise

Men understand there's nothing desperate about letting people know what you want. There are several ways to let the world know that you're in the market for a date, from discreet word-of-mouth to bold billboards that advertise the wonder that is you. Pick the method that best suits your personality and needs.

PERSONAL ADS

Men use personal ads more than women do, which is why a simple ad placed by a female can result in a mailbox full of prospective suitors.

And if someone tries to tell you that only losers use the personals, ask them if they've ever combed the classifieds for a job. Same thing, baby. You're not risking your life meeting people this way. Most of the people who place or answer ads are professionals who are too busy to hang out in bars or depend on chance to meet someone. Remember what I said about men and investments? If he's spent the money to take out an ad, he's serious about getting a return on his investment.

But it helps if you think like a man before and after to place or answer an ad. Here are some tips that I teach in my seminars and coaching sessions for getting the greatest response.

Be Specific

Men like to cut to the chase. Use precise words that describe what you're looking for. If you say "tall," do you mean over six feet or taller than you? The more specific you are, the better your chances of finding a compatible date. Remember, you are only looking for dates at this point, not soulmates. This will take the pressure off your search, and it won't scare men who are trying to avoid the bridal brigade.

Before writing your ad, take out your "Wants" and "Needs" lists. Select the five most important traits from those lists having to do with his career, education, religion and lifestyle. Now look at your profile of America's Most Wanted. Use this to describe his physical attributes such as height, weight, race and hair color.

If you're not getting enough of a response, ask a friend to critique your ad. You might also try to expand your search. Use national and local publications and online dating services such as Match.com and American Singles that reach all over the world. I promise that you will get stacks of letters and e-mails.

As you know, men are quite specific about their wants and needs, so you must include information about yourself as well. In order of importance, men are interested in:

1. Age, Height and Weight. Women lie about their age and weight, men lie about their height and salaries. You may think these stats should be irrelevant, but they are the first thing a man will look for in a personal ad. Be honest. You know you would prefer a tall, handsome, financially successful man to answer your ad over a short, bald burger flipper.

If you're over forty or fat, stay away from numbers. Euphemisms are your friends. Use terms like *boomer babe, sexy senior, ample, voluptuous, zaftig* or *BBW* (Big Beautiful Woman) instead. I suggest going directly to personals that cater to men looking for mature or larger-sized women. Check out the BBW sites on the Web. If you're forty-plus, you probably won't get as many responses as women in their twenties and thirties. Fact of life, baby. If you're blonde and in your twenties, better alert the post office—your mailbox is gonna be full!

It's not quantity you're looking for, it's quality. It takes only one good letter. Try magazines read by older folk like the *New York Review of Books*. CompuServe has a 40+ Singles Conference every Monday at 10:00 P.M., EST, and AOL has a site for boomers.

2. A Recent Photo. This is crucial to most men. They wouldn't buy a car before kicking the tires first. Most men won't date you sight unseen, even if his face would frighten small children and horses. Fact is, women read profiles, men look at pictures.

3. Hobbies. Men are curious about what you do outside of work. The more active you are, the better. If you're looking for intellectual men, the more mentally active you are, the better. Whatever you do, don't forget to include a hobby or two.

4. Smoking or Nonsmoking. (This is important to both genders.) Smokers like hanging out with other smokers because they feel persecuted by the anti-tobacco people (many of whom are ex-smokers), and because they can share the pleasure of a good puff.

5. Race/Religion. While this is an issue for some men, many would be willing to cross multicultural boundaries for the right woman. If this is a vital issue for you, however, make sure you mention this in your ad. If you have Internet access, you might also want to visit NetNoir, Latino or Jewish Singles on America Online or try the Single Christian Network.

6. Occupation. This is the least important item for men. If they love you, men don't care if you count paper clips for a living. Some men are willing to date strippers, but they probably wouldn't bring them home to meet Mom.

Here are some ads placed by a few of my former clients (male and female) that worked:

Good morning, sweetheart! How long have you been waiting to hear these words? How often have you longed to be awakened by a sweet, gentle kiss from a woman who is financially independent, affectionate, grounded and open to unlimited possibilities?

I'm a fit 5'4", and I'm able to make you a morning brew and breakfast that will knock your socks off. If this appeals to you, perhaps you are my beloved. If you are 6', between 30 and 45, a generous, gracious, attractive, loving, nonsmoking, drug-free, one-woman man who is interested in a committed meaningful relationship, this former radio producer would like to meet you. Photo please

Head-turning, accomplished, creative, cerebral, spiritual, romantic Renaissance woman with a true sense of what's important in life. Enjoy exploring city and country. Seek confident, highly creative, accomplished, kindred spirit who lives life with grace. Nonsmoker and social drinker only. 40-plus Note/Photo

Tall, dark and handsome, funny, successful Roman Catholic man, 27, down-to-earth business owner with integrity, who enjoys movies, reading, good wine, adventure biking and nature, a great basketball game on the weekend and a BBQ with neighbors. Seek intelligent, shapely, loving woman, 25–30, with a warm smile and great sense of humor for a relationship that will lead to marriage.

Brainy, sincere, elegant, very attractive (30, 5'7") woman of color. Avid skier, tennis player, runner and well-traveled professional. Seek very intelligent, optimistic, tactful, cosmopolitan, successful gentleman. Honesty, sincerity, kindness and a sense of humor are also important. No disease/drugs/drinkers/smokers. Photo Please.

Handsome Italian doctor, 36, 6'4" seeks single female, any race, 29–37, who is also professional, financially independent, well traveled, athletic and passionate about life. Should be comfortable in jeans as well as formal evening gown. Let's be friends then lovers, and work toward a long-term relationship (Note/Photo)

It's a good idea to read a lot of ads before you place one. Start with the periodicals in your area. You'll pick up the shorthand and get to know what it is that attracts you to certain ads. It'll also give you concrete evidence that there are sane single folk out there just like you who are sincere in their search for romance.

- **Highlight the ads that hook you, from both sexes.** Ask yourself what it was about the ads you selected that made them stand out. Did they have attention-grabbing words that make men want to read on, such as, "I can cook, too!" "Madonna lookalike" or "Your mom is going to be happy when you take me home"?
- **Keep it light.** Men just want to have fun. If you're witty, show them why it would be a hoot to take you out on a date. Avoid sappy, girly clichés like "long walks on the beach" and "cuddling by the fireside." Men like to do these things, too, but they want to be seduced, not romanced into calling you.
- **Show your ad to a male friend.** Ask him to honestly critique it. Whatever you do, don't show it to a parent or family member who will be hypercritical. You need support as well as healthy criticism. It doesn't hurt to show it to someone who writes or edits for living. They'll be able to edit your ad so it sings on the page.

After you place or post your ad, don't worry if you don't like the first batch of responses you get. Some men hang onto publications for a while before reading them. The mail will probably keep on coming for several weeks.

Do the right thing, however, and respond to everyone who writes you. If he's taken the time to send you a letter and photo, the least you can do is to send him a thank-you note. How would you feel if a man didn't bother to answer your letters? Tell them (lie) that you recently met someone and wish them luck in their search.

Once you've selected your top candidates, call them! Tell them you liked their letter or e-mail, and that you want to meet in person. Always meet in a public place, and take your own car or transportation. Tell a friend where, when and who you're going to meet. If you get a strange feeling that the guy on the phone is a freak, DON'T SEE HIM. Trust your gut, and tell him that you don't think you two would make a good match.

I recommend meeting for a cup of coffee during the day. Do not have alcohol, because it can impede your judgment. This way, if it's not going well, you can order an espresso. If you like the guy, you can always linger over a cappuccino.

Also, have an escape plan ready. After 45 minutes, look at your watch and say, "I'm meeting my friend/workmate/sister. Thanks so much for coming. I enjoyed meeting you." Say this whether you want to see the guy again or not. If you like him, tell him that you've got to run, but you'd love to get together again. Give him your voice mail number that is not connected to your home.

Don't be discouraged if the first few guys you meet turn out to be bombs. Remember, darlin', it's a numbers game. It's an interview. Personals are just another way to date, date, date!

ANSWERING AN AD

If you see an ad you like, answer it right away. Some men run ads for up to six months, so you'll have to take a number if you wait too long. This is another reason why placing an ad is better than answering one. Isn't it better to be the one who's picking and choosing, rather than number 185 on the supermarket line?

Like your ad, your letter should be light and breezy. Don't give everything away in your first missive. Leave some mystery, but give him some information that you can talk about when he calls.

If he asks for a photo, get one professionally done so you

look your best. Unless you are naturally photogenic, it's worth the expense. All you need is one good pix and 100 copies. No eight-by-tens, honey, you're not looking for a role on Broadway. And no lingerie shots, unless you're interested in a sex partner.

If he doesn't ask for a photo, send him a postcard with a picture that has meaning to you. Use personal stationery that is elegant or monogrammed; brighter colors will also make your letter stand out from the pack. No flowers, animals or cutesy stamps. And no perfumed paper. Those days are over.

Do not send form letters. Even if you use the same paragraph to describe yourself, tailor your response to the ad you've selected. Mention something that he wrote, such as, "I am also a skier. Have you ever been to Vail?"

When the guy calls you in response to your letter, keep the conversation short. Save the long talk for your first meeting. Go to the coffee shop carrying the publication that featured the ad. Try to relax. He's just as nervous as you are, and it's only an hour of your time.

If he's not exactly who he said he was, so what? Nobody's perfect, and even men exaggerate about their height and salaries. Don't confront him about these peccadilloes when you meet. If you're not interested in a second date, thank him for coffee and cross him off your list.

DATING SERVICES

If you follow my strategy, you will not need a dating service. Why pay thousands of dollars to a service when you can do the same thing for yourself?

Now that many people have computers, there are sites where you can scan through hundreds of pictures and member profiles to select someone who sounds compatible. They are safe as long as you don't use your real name or give out your address or vital information. Once you've checked him out, talked to him on the phone, and know where he works, you can meet in a public place.

Services like Match.com and American Singles are legitimate well-staffed businesses that do some of the legwork for you. You can target your search from three blocks to 3,000 miles away.

Singles events that involve going out to lunch or going to restaurants are great, because you're essentially group dating and doing something else that you enjoy while meeting new people. One-on-one matchmakers are also good, because you will get more personal attention.

BUSINESS CARDS

Remember the networking days of the eighties? Business cards are no longer a novelty, they're a necessity. Even if you already have one, get a personal card that has your name, voice mail number and no address.

Keep it simple and have it professionally designed and embossed. You can also add your e-mail address and screen name if you're online. Avoid using cheesy-looking clip art. You should always carry these cards with you, because you never know who you might meet.

BILLBOARDS

Looking for an adventurous way to get a man's attention? If you follow some basic safety rules, this method isn't as risky as it sounds. Men know the power of the written word, especially when those words are six feet long! This isn't for everyone, in fact, it isn't for most women, but there have been several men who successfully advertised for dates by taking out an ad on a billboard. All of them met their future wives this way.

It sounds desperate, because it is. You have to have the means and the *cojones* to do this. I don't recommend using a billboard as a way to gather prospective dates, but I do think a billboard might work if you have a specific man in mind whose attention you want to get.

Your ad might read: "Bill Thomas, what are you waiting for? Give me a call so I can show you why we are made for each other! Love, Ginnie." Don't put your last name or phone number on the billboard. People all over town will be buzzing, and your man will be so flattered that he'll *have* to call you. If you're the outrageous type, go for it!

First, Second and Third Date Game Plans

My clients are always asking me if there is a game plan for the first, second and third dates. Well, baby, you know I don't believe in the three-dates-before-sex equation, but I do think there is a strategy that women should follow during the kick-off, so to speak.

To switch metaphors for a moment, a healthy relationship starts with the foundation that is formed on the first three dates. The stronger the foundation, the stronger the relationship will be in the long run. Every date from then on is another beam, bolt, concrete block and architectural flourish.

Here is a basic blueprint for you to follow.

BE PREPARED

When it comes to dating, you've got to be prepared. Make sure you get a good night's sleep. I like to put on some dance music while I'm getting ready for a date to get into an upbeat mood.

I often take a long bath beforehand and enjoy a glass of wine or a cup of mint tea to calm my nerves. While in the bath, take some deep clarifying breaths and start imagining yourself having a good time. These images will help you mentally prepare by rehearsing the date. Repeat "I'm going to have fun" to yourself whenever you start to feel anxious. This will also develop a positive mental attitude and build your self-confidence.

THE FIRST DATE

On the first date you should go out for coffee or lunch. Never go out on a Friday or Saturday for a first date. Keep it casual. If you meet for lunch, you always have work obligations as an excuse if the date is a bust. And if you're having fun, you can always agree to meet again.

Men use first dates for checking you out, not for instant romance. Love at first sight happens about as often as Haley's Comet. On your first date, keep an eye out for red flags or sparks caused by physical chemistry.

Be yourself. You're checking each other out, but you don't need to work at it to impress him. He's not looking to be swept off his feet by you—that's your romantic ideal, not his. Take time to get to know your date, and allow him to get to know the real you.

The beauty of a lunch date is that it's not conducive to getting you into bed after the bill is presented. You go your separate but equal ways. It doesn't matter if he's picked up the check. There's no quid pro quo based on the money he's spent in the last hour. If he wants to make a second date, tell him to call you later. Don't take your appointment book out just yet. This way, if you're not interested, you can tell him on the phone rather than embarrassing him to his face.

It also gives you more time to make an assessment. Is there any possibility of a friendship? Did you want to learn more about him? Pay close attention to your gut reactions. Was there something about him that bothered you?

Men will put several days between the first and second

dates, especially if the first date went really well. They like to give themselves time to sit back and evaluate how they feel. They know that waiting to call you sends a message that they have a life outside of dating, or that they're seeing other women. Either way, it shows that he's not desperate. Neither are you, girlfriend!

THE SECOND DATE

On your second date, go out for dinner. Give yourself more time to gather information about your date. Don't go to a movie where you spend two hours sitting silently in the dark. You should be talking, talking, talking.

If you like the finer things in life and he asks you to pick the restaurant, choose the best restaurant in town. This lets him know that your standards are high. If he tells you it's out of his price range, that's okay: you've sent a message about what you aspire to.

Again, when a man is doing business, he's going to take the client to a good restaurant or get tickets to the hottest show or sporting event. A date with you should be important enough to a man to part with a little cash.

If you hate formal dining, go to a Sunday brunch or someplace where you can unwrap your food together. This sends another message about the kind of person you are.

THE THIRD DATE

The third date is the key, because it's the one in which you decide whether or not you want to continue seeing each other. If there are three strikes against him after the third date, he's out of your dating lineup.

If you're still not sure and you want to give him another chance, you can always pull him out again (i.e., date him again in the future) in between your other dates who have moved up ahead of him. Sounds cold? It's not. It's just the way the game is played, baby.

You might want to keep a scorecard, especially if you're dating more than two men. He may have hit one out of the park when he showed up with flowers. Maybe he asked the waiter to uncork the restaurant's best wine. Extra points. Perhaps he lost a few points when he made you wait fifteen minutes before arriving, or talked to his broker on the cell phone during lunch.

Rate your dates as if you were a coach looking at the strengths and weaknesses of his players. "Good arm," a coach might note, "but he's a slow runner." Your dating scorecard should read something like, "Mike is smart, funny, but a bit of a braggart." Or, "Tom is not quite over his ex." The way he rates will determine whether or not he gets another date.

Here are some warning signs that will help you keep score:

- **Excessive questioning.** Do his questions have jealous overtones about your past or other current relationships? This could be an early warning sign of possessiveness.
- **Time commitments not honored.** Is he chronically late? Does he change plans at the last minute? Does he not call when he says he will?
- **Excessive need to be in control of dates.** Does he display hurt or anger when you assert your own preferences? If you tell him you'd prefer lunch for the first date, does he insist on an evening date? Also, take note: Does he belittle or ignore your suggestions, or override them with his own?
- **Abusive treatment of service staff.** Does he snap his fingers to get a waiter's attention, unnecessarily send back food or complain to the manager? This can be a sign of an abusive personality. Pay attention to his statements about women. Does he use the word "bitch" a lot?

- **Alcohol/drug abuse.** Does he drink to excess on your first few dates? Does he tell stories about his druggy days or look bleary-eyed during your date? Does he sniff a lot and seem jumpy?
- **Racist remarks.** This can be in the form of jokes or demeaning comments about other people.
- **"Forgets" his wallet.** Did he conveniently forget his wallet on a date, or suggest that you go dutch?
- **Sexual remarks.** This includes unsavory jokes, double entendres or references to body parts.
- **Unwanted sexual advances.** Did he touch you inappropriately or make you feel uncomfortable or threatened?
- **Wandering eyes.** Does he make eye contact with you while talking, or is he busy looking at other women in the room? Does he constantly gaze at himself in the mirror?

DOUBLE AND GROUP DATING

More and more people are going out in groups rather than the traditional one-on-one date. Group dating is great because it takes some of the pressure off two people meeting for the first time. You have other people to talk to, so you can feel more relaxed. It also slows down the process a bit, and gives you more time to get to know each other.

This is especially good for people who are shy. Once you feel comfortable with the people around you, you can have the courage to go one-on-one. This is the only situation where I think it's good for everyone to pay his or her own way. If it's a double date, the man should pay, but in a group of eight, everyone should split the check evenly.

The only danger in double dating with a girlfriend is the tendency to fall back on the security of an old friendship. You might find yourself talking to each other rather than to your dates. And since you have so much history, you will probably make references and private jokes about things that your dates don't understand. This is rude and exclusionary, and it will only sabotage your experience.

Men Are Fluent in Body Language

Flirting is adult play, and men like to play hard. If you are following this program, you will be surrounded by men who are vying for your company. That doesn't mean that men don't need a little push every now and then. Flirting is one of the great joys in life, and it's something we should do even after we are in a relationship.

Some of the best flirts in the world are little kids. If you want to learn how to be coquettish, watch how children get their parents to buy them a toy or candy. I first realized that flirting was fun when I was four years old. I was running for Miss Milk Fund, where I had to collect money to buy milk for underprivileged children.

My aunt took me to neighborhood stores to ask adults to contribute to the fund. One day she took me into a barbershop, which was filled with men. She sat me on a chair all dressed up in my Sunday best. I had these little sunglasses that I would pull down and wink at all the customers. I don't know where I learned this, but it seemed to come naturally to me.

The men in the barbershop were beside themselves. They told my aunt, "Whatever she's collecting for, I want to be a part of it." Needless to say, I won the contest hands down.

The point of the story is, men love women who flirt. The first thing that you have to do is smile. It lights up your face and tells others that you are happy and accessible. Smiling is a way of breaking down that wall and letting people know that you're approachable. The right eye contact and a bright smile can send a man sailing in your direction like a heat-seeking missile.

As we get older, we become bogged down with serious issues such as careers, money and family stress. I'm not saying that you should walk around grinning like the village idiot, but a ready smile when you meet someone will make people want to be around you.

I had a girlfriend once who was attractive but miserable. Every time we'd go out together, she would have a sour puss on that repelled men faster than spraying a can of Raid on insects. Men would actually approach her, not to ask her out, but to ask her what was bothering her. They'd pat her on the shoulder and say, "It's not that bad, honey" or "Who died?" This is not the kind of attention you want.

If you want to see how you appear to others, spend some time smiling at yourself in the mirror. Are you a half-smiler? Do you grin from ear to ear? You'll feel silly at first, but it's important to see how the world views you.

Practice smiling until you look like someone you would like to talk to. Have a friend take photographs of you smiling, and ask a *male* friend to tell you what kind of impression you make. You may be surprised by what you find out.

In addition to smiling, another great way to flirt is to express genuine interest in what a man is saying. You don't have to laugh at his jokes if they're not funny, but make sure you respond to what is being said. Listening can be an aphrodisiac to many men.

Also, pay attention to what you're wearing when you're at a party or singles event. A suit is great for work, but dating shouldn't be work—it should be fun! If you really want to be approached by a guy, casual dress is better. Men are intimidated by women who are too formal. It makes them think of their mothers, and events that they don't really want to go to.

Men like to be comfortable. This is why they have that favorite pair of boxers that they wear until they disintegrate. You don't always have to wear makeup and a mini to attract a man (although guys *love* miniskirts!). If a man tries to pick you up at the laundromat when you're in your sweats and T-shirt, he *really* likes you.

It's fun to dress up when you're going out, but you shouldn't have to hide the homegirl inside you if you're out for a Sunday brunch. But always make sure your clothes are clean, pressed and flattering to your figure.

Unless you're onstage or on the beach, you should never dress too revealingly. Women who dress seductively in order to attract a man will get sex, but they won't necessarily get intimacy or a long-term relationship. Men like mystery, so if you're exposing too much of yourself, you are denying them the pleasure of using their imagination.

Flirting is also knowing how to initiate a conversation. When I do TV talk shows, the hosts sometimes ask me to go behind the scenes with a hidden mike and camera and instruct a woman from the audience on how to flirt. I'll tell her to ask a question like, "Do you know a good bookstore in the neighborhood?" or "I'm new in town, can you recommend some restaurants?"

I'll tell her to smile, flip her hair, be gracious and polite. By the end of the session, the woman will have a date for the evening. It's never failed.

Asking a man for advice makes him feel important and helpful. The next time you're in a store, ask a male shopper for help buying a tie for your father or brother. It doesn't matter what you ask, as long as you engage him in conversation. If he doesn't want to be helpful, say, "Thanks anyway," and move on.

Elevators are another great place to flirt with men. I do this all the time. If I find myself alone with a cute guy I'll say, "I'm so glad there's a man on this elevator, because I get so scared when I'm by myself. Now I can hold onto you." Men just light up when I say this! They just love feeling as though they're protecting you.

If you're in a café, you can ask, "What's the best coffee

they make here?" If you're online, ask a man where the best chat rooms are.

Of course, it is disrespectful to flirt with other men when you are out on a date. If some guy is flirting with me while he's with another woman, I'll tell him, "You have a beautiful girlfriend. Does she know you're hitting on other women? You'd better go pay attention to her before some other guy steals her away." This usually does the trick.

According to Jan Hargrave's must-read book, *Let Me See Your Body Talk* (Kendall/Hunt), psychologists studying American daters identified a "courtship dance" that leads from the initial meeting to a relationship.

In order for the courtship to be successful, Hargrave explains, the man must wait for an appropriate signal from his partner before moving to the next step of the dance. When the male holds the female's hand, for example, he must wait until she presses his hand before attempting the next step, which is entwining his fingers with hers.

Men and women label each another "slow" or "fast" depending on how they move through this dance. Those who skip a few steps are considered "fast."

You can attract more men than you can handle by simply perfecting the art of body language. Here are some tips that I teach my clients and students. If the body talks, baby, men will listen:

- Develop a graceful but confident sort of walk, one that is free and easy, with fluid movements. This kind of walk sends a message that will turn a man's head!
- Stand with one hand on your hip. Translation: "I dare you to come talk to me!"
- Cross and uncross your legs when you're wearing a dress. I'm talking Sharon Stone in *Basic Instinct* with panties on. Nothing is sexier to a man.
- Let your eyes linger on his eyes while you're talking. An

initial gaze of around three seconds is best, and you should smile immediately upon making eye contact.

- Wet your lips with your tongue. I guarantee you that this will make any man feel uneasy as well as excited, and put you in control.
- Reapply your lipstick.
- Toss or flip your hair. Hair flipping and twisting may seem like a nervous tic, but it's actually a way of saying that you want to be approached.
- With artfully dropped eyelids, hold a man's gaze, then quickly look away. The feeling of being peeped at can light a fire in a man's heart.
- The slight exposure of the shoulder from a partially fallen blouse is another fine example of flirting.
- Massage your neck with one hand. It has the effect of raising the breast on one side of the body. It also exposes the armpit, which is erotic.
- Expose the smooth, soft skin of your wrists. The wrist is considered a highly erotic area.
- Play with any cylindrical object such as a pencil, pen or the stem of a wineglass. This reveals your subconscious desires.
- Sit with one leg tucked under the other and pointed toward the man you want to attract.
- With crossed legs, gently kick your top leg back and forth. This kicking or thrusting is another courting signal.
- Dangle one shoe while seated in a relaxed position with one leg crossed over the other at the knee.

Several years ago, psychologist Monica Moore (no relation) did a study on women who flirt. She identified several common flirting behaviors, some of which I've already mentioned. I've chosen others from her list that I've seen work. Study this list and mine above, and use at least three of these techniques the next time you want to attract a man:

Facial/Head Pattern

Smile
Room-encompassing glance
Laugh
Head nod
Giggle
Whisper
Neck exposure
Pout
Coy smile
Eyebrow arch

Posture Patterns

Dancing by yourself
Accepting an offer to dance
Asking for help
Knee, shoulder, arm touch
Hug

Gestures

Gesticulation
Primping
Hand-holding
Caressing face or hair
Hiking skirt (just a little)

Remember that your body language will make the difference between someone approaching you or not. If you have your arms folded, you are saying, "I'm a closed person, so stay away." Touching your heart with your hand says you're trustworthy. Cradling your chin in your hand says you are a good listener.

If you slouch and your chest and shoulders fall forward, you will look concave. You are telling people that you're shy or introverted. Always maintain good posture (not soldier-straight, but erect and chest out). Above all, feeling comfortable in your own body is nature's best calling card.

I'm not saying you should affect these postures if they don't come naturally, but be aware of what your body is saying when you're out on a date.

Men Like to Flirt, Too

Flirtation is a two-way street, and men do it almost as much as women do. Keep in mind that in the animal world, it's the male that struts his stuff in order to attract the female, not the other way around.

Here are some common male flirting techniques. With practice you can learn to recognize these signals easily so they can help you determine in advance if a man is interested:

- Partly unbuttoned shirt, loosened tie.
- Sitting with his legs wide open.
- Sucking his stomach in and pushing his chest out.
- A strong, determined walk, like John Travolta in *Saturday Night Fever*.
- Cologne that is musky and not too strong. (No man wears cologne unless he's trolling.)
- Standing with one hand on his hip, with his hip thrust forward. Says, "I'm a strong man." (My three-year-old godson has already mastered this one.)
- Standing with head cocked slightly at an angle.
- Self-grooming such as adjusting his tie, fiddling with the collar, or hand combing his hair.
- Carrying a prop, such as a travel magazine, newspaper or a book. A man will use the prop to start up a conversation with a woman. It is much easier to talk about something rather than approach a woman unarmed.

- Slowly buttoning and unbuttoning or zipping and unzipping the jacket, indicating slight nervousness, or taking the jacket off completely.
- Playing with objects. Squeezing, then letting go. Translation: I want to squeeze you.
- Glancing at a woman's bod, and letting her see him do it.
- Sock-pulling. When men are nervous in the presence of a woman, they tend to pull their socks up.
- Lightly stroking either his outer or, less often, inner thigh.
- The thumbs-in-belt "cowpoke" stance. This is accomplished when one or both thumbs are hooked into the pockets with fingers pointing toward the groin area.
- Sly winks, accidental touches or leaning toward you.

THE ROLE REVERSAL

One of best ways to learn how to think like a man is to engage in a little role-playing. Enlist a girlfriend to go with you to a singles bar or party.

Pretend you are a man who wants to ask a woman out on a date. Look around the room for women you would feel comfortable striking up a conversation with. What about them attracts you? Are they pretty? Well dressed? Do they smile a lot and seem friendly and open?

You'll find that the prettiest woman in the room might not be the one you'd choose to talk to first. She may be projecting an attitude that says, "Speak to me at your own risk." No one likes being rejected, so the person you find most appealing will probably be the one who appears to be the most welcoming.

This exercise will help you to understand what a woman can do to make a difficult social situation a little easier. And it will definitely increase your chances of being approached by men the next time you're looking to be picked up.

Men Like Real Breasts

Cosmetic surgery can be wonderful if it changes the way you feel about yourself. I had a breast reduction many years ago, and I couldn't be happier. Now I don't get unwanted attention, and my body feels better proportioned. And when the time comes, if I want to, I'll get something else nipped or tucked.

If you can afford it, go for it. But don't do it for anyone except yourself. If you're dating a man who asks you go from a B to a D, give him an F. A man shouldn't love you for the size of your breasts. Say, "Sure, honey, I'll get implants, as soon as you add a few more inches between your legs."

The truth is, men may fantasize about the big-breasted women, but when the bras come off, they want to feel what's real.

Men Like Hair They Can Touch

Most men prefer women to have long hair, and blondes do have more fun in the dating world. But if you have hair that's mousy brown and grows out instead of down, don't stress. Use a highlight to jazz up your color, and get a femnine-looking short cut. Just avoid the ducktails and buzz cuts if it's men you're interested in attracting.

Invest in a professional hairstylist and colorist—it's worth it. They will tell you what cut and color work best for your face. This is a luxury that every woman should afford herself.

Stay away from hairspray and gels that give you that helmet-head or gunky look. You're not a sculpture; your hair should move when you do. Also, don't choose a dye that is too far from your natural color. Of course, if magenta hair works with your lifestyle, you can go with any color of the rainbow. But most men don't like fake-looking hair.

Only go blonde if you can pull it off. Bottle blondes are as easy to spot as men with rugs.

The exception to the natural rule is coloring over gray hair. I have a friend who started going prematurely gray at age thirty. I encouraged her to color her hair because she was too young to be snow-white. She finally gave in, and it totally changed her personality. There's time enough to be distinguished—color while you're still young.

Girlfriend, I know that hair is extremely important to you, but it shouldn't rule your life. When you're having a bad hair day, don't inflict your self-conscious misery on your dates. Stay home, or put a damn bag over your head.

Men Like Long Nails, Not Claws

I'm sorry, honey, but if you can't punch a telephone without using a pencil head, your nails are too long. Nails that walk into a room before you do are like signs saying point me to the trailer park.

Men love simply polished, well-manicured, not-bitten-to-the-nub nails. Sparkles, decals and unusual colors are great for teenagers. Stick to the red, pink and coral family. French tips can be lovely on the right kind of nails; fake tips are not. Men don't want things falling off your body when they touch them! If a nail breaks, cut them all down and start over.

Men Respond to Color

I live in New York, where the preferred dress code is black with a touch of black. The basic black number is a wonderful, failproof choice, especially for an evening event. But if you want to stand out from the crowd, honey, wear red!

I've always been a person of color, so when a client told me she was going to a housewarming party. I helped her select a sexy red outfit instead of the little black number she was going to wear. She told me afterward that she got more attention from both men *and* women than she had ever gotten in her life. People went up to her at the party and said, "You look so beautiful in that dress!" To this day, men remember her as the woman in the red dress.

Avoid wearing pink, yellow, lace, flowers and pastels. These kinds of colors and frills are for little girls or grannies. The same goes for sweaters that have things sewn on them, like animals, decals or God knows what else. Men are simple dressers, and women should be, too.

The only exception to the pastel rule is when you're meeting his parents. In that case, dress as if you're going to a wedding. The more conservative, the better.

Shop with a friend whose taste you trust to see what colors work best for you. Don't get too caught up in trends. Buy one trendy thing a season and that's it. You probably won't wear that animal-print coat again, but the classic sweater will be in your closet forever.

Don't throw your trendy clothes away, however, because you never know when they will come back in style. (Hello, bell bottoms, Capri pants, clogs and wrap dresses.) Years from now, we'll probably be wearing hoop skirts again.

A Man Will Show You When He's Not Interested

Just as men will show you with their bodies when they're interested, they will let you know when they aren't open to being approached.

For example, when a man is sitting or standing with his arms crossed, it usually means he does not want to be approached and probably doesn't care to listen to what you have to say.

He may also be frustrated and lonely, so these body clues alone might not be enough of a deterrent. Take a look at his expression. Is he tense and frowning? If so, don't go near this guy. He's the Greta Garbo of men—he wants to be left alone.

Men who are unattractive or poorly dressed lack self-confidence. They usually just stand around bashfully on the sidelines staring at the ground or watching other people having fun. In essence, these men are saying, "Please find someone else to talk to."

If you want to rescue these guys, go ahead. They will be eternally grateful, and they might even have a great personality behind that grimace. And who knows? It might be worth the effort to coax them out of their shells, especially if you are the shy type yourself.

Men Don't Approach Women Who Travel in Packs

I don't care what anyone says, a man's biggest fear is of being rejected. When you're out at a party, club or social event, only take one girlfriend with you. Do not hang out in packs. Who wants to ask a woman out when there's a protective posse waiting to give you the once-over?

Make a pact with your friend to work different parts of the room and meet at the door at a prearranged time. Being by yourself makes you so much more approachable. Remember, you're there to attract men, not to be with your girlfriend. Do the girlfriend thing another day.

Men Don't Like Too Much Perfume

Remember the commercial, "Your Windsong stays on my mind"? Well, honey, any perfume that follows you into a room and stays there long after you are gone is too damn much. There's nothing worse than being in an elevator with some woman who smells like she's just taken a bath in her perfume bottle.

The truth is, men prefer women who smell clean and natural. We are all animals, after all, and men respond well to the scent of the female. If you must wear a fragrance, spray it away from your body and walk through the mist. That's it. Or put a dab on your pressure points. If you have good grooming skills, your personal aroma will draw a man to you.

Men Don't Like Too Much Jewelry

Too much jewelry is like too much fragrance. It's distracting. Making noise when you walk into a room or reflecting light like a disco ball is embarrassing and ostentatious. One simple necklace, a string of pearls or diamond stud earrings is all you need. When it comes to jewelry, it's about quality, not quantity.

Besides, you want your date to concentrate on what you're saying, not the hula hoops dangling from your ears. The focus should be on you. Save the expensive jewelry for a formal occasion.

The same goes for body jewelry. When you're in your teens, ten earrings on each ear and a pierced nose can look cool. As you get older, you want to avoid puncture wounds. But here, once again, it's all about who you want to attract. If you want your man to be well pierced, go for the gold.

PART V

How to Have Sex Like a Man: Sex Tips from Men That You Can't Live/Date Without

If men are Masters of the Universe, as writer Tom Wolfe suggested, their satellite planets are sex and money.

One reason men know so much about sex is because they've been doing it longer than we have. According to the Janus Report on Sexual Behavior, 21 percent of the men interviewed said they've had sexual intercourse by the age of fourteen, compared to 15 percent of women.

By examining how men think about sex and what they like and don't like, you will start having more fun in bed. Forget about the politically correct, therapeutic bull that you get from other sex guides for women. Having good sex is easy: Don't think so damn much and start *feeling*.

Anything goes as long as you are safe, consensual and don't involve children or animals. If you don't know what it means to have safe sex by now, I know an island in the South Pacific where you should live out the rest of your life—alone. It's simple: Don't have sex until you've been tested for AIDS and STDs. Period.

Men Know the Difference Between Love and Lust

As soon as you start having sex with a man, you must ask yourself several questions: Is he sleeping with you exclusively? Is sex the major part of your relationship, or do you eat and go to a movie every once in a while? Does he call you only when he's horny?

A booty call is when a man dials you up at 3:00 A.M., tells you he's thinking about you, dreaming about you, and asks if you would mind coming over for a little snuggle time. Women who are interested in a serious commitment should not accept the booty call. Booty calls are not dates. They are appointments to have sex.

Men will do anything for sex; they'll even risk losing their job and family (remember President Clinton and Monica Lewinsky?). A woman, on the other hand, will do anything for a relationship. She'll sleep with a married man, support a deadbeat or get slapped around and verbally abused. Women will also risk losing their friends and family if they are "in love" with a man.

If you find yourself in any of these situations, call a therapist the next time you feel like calling your boyfriend.

Men Will Have Sex Anywhere

Most men, if given the choice, prefer to be on their own turf. But when it comes to sex, anyplace will do, be it a bedroom, bathroom, hallway or kitchen floor.

That being the case, once you get to the stage where you're having sex, you should split the time you are together between your place and his. The first time, however, I recommend not inviting him to your home or apartment. This way, if the relationship doesn't work out, you won't have the memory of him in your bedroom.

The Cherokee Indians believe that every time you have someone in your bed, his spirit stays there. You don't want to change your mattress every time a man sleeps over! You have to be really careful about who you let into your home, not to mention your bed. These are your sacred places. The first few times, make him provide a romantic space for you, even if it means going to a hotel.

Men Are Selfish About Sex

Until fairly recently, most men couldn't care less if a woman had an orgasm. Like the Romans, they came, they saw, they conquered, though not necessarily in that order. Men have since learned that sex is a lot better when both parties are enjoying themselves. They discovered that they get even more turned on by the sight of a women being turned on. Good news for us.

But they also know that it's okay to be selfish in bed, at least part of the time. Sex is give-and-take. Sometimes you give, sometimes you get. Like the jingle in the movie theater says: Sit back, relax and enjoy the show. Your man will let you know when it's time for you to get back onstage and start performing.

Men Like Women Who Are Fit

You've waited for months and you are now ready (dying) to do the nasty. You're emotionally prepared for the big step to the next level of your relationship, and you want to be physically prepared as well.

Sex is like any sport. Sure, some people are natural athletes, but you can always get better if you train. Training requires eating right, exercising regularly and practice (having more sex!). Being good at sex takes trial and error, especially if you want to go for the gold. You'll eventually learn what techniques and positions you play best.

Good sex also requires getting fit, which means being healthy, not anorexic-thin. Nowadays, hard bodies and good muscle tone are in vogue (body trends change almost every decade), but there are plenty of men who like soft and curvy.

It's important to be physically active as much for your health as for your body.

Lifting free weights or using the Cybex machines at the gym will not make you look like Arnold Schwarzenegger. Building muscle actually helps you lose inches by burning up fat. Having a sculpted body will also add to your feeling of well-being and power.

Of course, you must include a cardio workout in your regular exercise regimen in order to maintain or lose weight. This can be anything from tennis to racquetball to basketball to running, as long as you don't get bored and go back to creasing the couch.

Some women like classes where they have an esprit de corps (other women who have the same goal in mind). Others like the freedom of running, which you can do anywhere. I promise that if you get your heart pumping on a regular basis, you'll get a man's heart pumping, too.

Don't beat yourself up trying to look like a personal trainer. I'll say it again, because women can't hear this enough—it's more important to be healthy than to be thin. If you're comfortable with your body—however tall, short, fat or flat it is—men will love it, too.

Men Like Blow Jobs

For men, sex without a blow job is like dining out without ordering a cocktail first. In fact, it's drinks, appetizer and dessert rolled into one. Some men, especially those who cheat on their wives, don't consider blow jobs sex. President Clinton spent more than a year proclaiming this on national television. My fellow Americans, if swallowing a man's dick isn't sex, I don't know what is.

Giving head can be fun because men love it so damn much and because *you* are in control of his pleasure. If you find this activity distasteful, guaranteed he will find someone who thinks his dick is a Cherry Garcia on a sugar cone. The truth is, honey, a man doesn't care who's down there. It could be a man, a robot or a succubus. All they know is that it feels good. Besides, he can't see your face anyway.

Jay Leno asked actor Hugh Grant what he was thinking when he flagged down a Hollywood hooker for a quick one in the car, when his model/girlfriend Elizabeth Hurley was waiting for him at home. I'll tell you. He wasn't *thinking*. When the penis and the brain do battle, guess who's the victor?

Get to Know Mr. Happy

Men have spent a lifetime getting to know their penises so, baby, you've got some catching up to do. Understand that men are obsessed with their schlongs, so never laugh when you first unwrap one. Act as if it comes in one of those lovely blue Tiffany boxes. Giggling will send a man straight to the Viagra jar.

The flaccid penis can be anywhere from two inches to seven, while the erect penis can range from just under four inches to just over ten. The average length of an erect penis is six inches. Once and for all, size doesn't matter when it comes to clitoral stimulation, but both men and women like big dicks.

According to Susan Bordo's book *The Male Body*, many men wish their cocks could be larger. Given the choice between being 5'2" with a seven-inch penis and being 6'2" with a two-incher, two-thirds of the guys chose being short and hung.

Kiss It, Lick It, Squeeze It, Tease It

Just about any verb you can think of works when it comes to penises. Try placing soft kisses on the shaft and head. Now lick the penis from base to tip, flicking your tongue on the underside of the tip. Some men like having their balls gently fondled or sucked ("tea bagging" involves placing the entire scrotum in your mouth), but don't have a Boston tea party down there—this is an extremely sensitive area.

Check in with him from time to time to see how it feels. Follow his directions, if he has any; he may want you to progress to some energetic sucking. If all he can do at this point is nod or groan, you're on the right track.

Kneel over him and take his erect penis lightly between the tips of your fingers, and let him see you smile provocatively before you touch the tip of your tongue to it. Swirl your tongue over its tip, and let your fingers slowly manipulate the smooth outer skin of his penis.

Take only the tip of it between your lips and hold it there as you increase the speed of your fingers. Make a fist around his shaft and move the fist up and down, with your breath playing over his flesh.

Use your lips and tongue to caress his shaft while rubbing him with your fingers. Either cover his penis with your mouth so at the last possible instant so you can capture the hot flow of his semen or let him come on your chest.

Deep Throating

Unless you're a sword-swallower, you probably have a limit to how much you can fit in your mouth. Don't worry; men know there are better places to put a penis than your throat. And gagging isn't the sexiest sound you can make.

When stimulating his penis, remember to wet it first with your tongue and saliva so your lips or hands will slide up and down the shaft more easily. Cover your teeth with your lips at all times, because this kind of reality bites. You might also like to have a can of whipped cream nearby for added incentive. It's worth the calories.

Men Like Women Who Swallow

Almost every porn flick will include a "come shot," which features smiling women with semen dripping from their face or lips. Why? Because men are proud of their little swimmers. Swallowing is, therefore, an act of love and acceptance for most men.

Whether you do or don't is your call. But keep in mind that semen is practically tasteless and that less than a teaspoon (the amount that's ejaculated) contains vitamin C, vitamin B12, sulfur, zinc and potassium. Hmmmmm.

The Moveable Feast

The good thing about pricks is they're portable, so you can go down on him just about anywhere. Blow jobs in cars are wonderful WHEN HE'S NOT DRIVING! This is why we have parking lots and scenic overlooks. This is also why some genius invented that little flap in the underpants. Unzip him before he gets out of his suit or pants and go to town. Be careful if you have bad knees.

Some Men Like Entering Through the Back Door

Not all men like anal sex, but many do. It's one reason some straight men are homophobic; they secretly like the idea of back door sex. The problem with anal sex is that it hurts. (Never, ever do this with anyone who hasn't tested negative for the HIV virus, and I mean look at his doctor's report—don't take his word for it!)

The bottom line here (sorry) is, do it if you like it. Butt (sorry, again) make sure you use lubrication such as K-Y jelly. If he's pressuring you to have anal sex against your will, tell him you'll try it as soon as he puts a baguette up his ass. (If his eyes light up, run for your life!)

Men Like to Watch

Men are visual creatures, and they're uninhibited when it comes to other people's bodies. Why do you think there are no stalls around urinals? To men, a dick is a dick is a dick (unless it's bigger than theirs, in which case it's a dick they wish they had).

One of the biggest turn-ons for men is to watch other people in flagrante. This can be done via a magazine or video, at a drunken frat party, or with an invited guest. There are even "swinging" magazines, which were really big in the seventies, that advertise for couples seeking other couples, and conventions where swingers can meet and swap.

If you're not into crowds (most women prefer one-on-one sex), you can use your imagination by pretending there's a third party in bed with you. Describe what that person is doing to you and him.

Some men like to videotape themselves having sex, or have mirrors on the ceiling or walls for extra visual stimulation. If you're the reflective type, get the kind of mirror that makes you look thinner, like the ones in department store dressing rooms. If not, you can let your man watch you while you masturbate. Men actually pay for this at peep shows!

Another treat for the voyeuristic man is to go to an upscale topless bar. While you're there, buy him a lap dance. This will cost between $10 and $20 for about three minutes of up-close and personal gyrations. Some dancers are allowed to actually sit in the man's lap, but all clubs have a strictly enforced hands-off policy. The dancers can touch the men—not vice versa. Should a man get fresh, a 250-pound bouncer will show him the door.

Believe me, honey, this is all in a day's work for the dancers, who are frequently beautiful (and surgically altered). Many of them are working mothers and college students trying to make a buck. At the best clubs, exotic dancers can make about $1,000 a night in tips. Sure, some of the women have drug habits, but so do some of the Wall Street guys who come to watch them.

The other men in the club will completely ignore you, and they will be jealous of your boyfriend for having such an open-minded partner. The service people will treat you with the utmost respect, and there's never a line in the ladies' room.

The greatest benefit, of course, is having your man all primed for a night of sex—with you! Don't worry that he's thinking about someone else while he's making love to you. She's not enjoying the fruits of his labor, you are!

Men Like to Masturbate

Okay, so you haven't been touched by an angel (or any human being, for that matter) in quite some time. You're either following my advice about waiting to have sex, or you haven't found anyone you'd like to get jiggy with.

Sexiest Movies

Need a video to get you in the mood for romance? Everyone has a favorite, but here are a few of mine:

***Romeo and Juliet* (1968)**

Zeffirelli's adaptation of the Shakespeare tragedy features two nubile actors as the star-crossed lovers. You have to be DOA not to cry at this one. And don't you dare rent the Leonardo DiCaprio version, no matter how many times you saw *Titanic*!

***Body Heat* (1981)**

A femme fatale (Kathleen Turner) lures a handsome lawyer (William Hurt) into murdering her rich husband. Turn on the AC, 'cause the torrid sex scene between Hurt and Turner will make you sweat.

***Risky Business* (1983)**

This rite-of-passage film introducing Tom Cruise is like *The Graduate* with call girls. It also contains some of the most women-pleasing scenes in modern cinematic history, namely: the young Cruise playing air-guitar in his jockeys; sex on a staircase with a high-class hooker (Rebecca De Mornay); and after-hours sex on the Chicago El.

***No Way Out* (1987)**

A Navy officer (Kevin Costner) gets involved with the mistress of the defense secretary. The paramour (Sean Young) is accidentally killed. She dies happy because before she goes, she has great sex in a limousine with Costner.

Well, baby, this doesn't mean that your life has to be totally sexless. Guys have been masturbating ever since Adam discovered his joystick! A 1996 sex survey conducted by *Men's Fitness* magazine found that 40 percent of the 1,158 men polled masturbate two or more times a week. Honey, that's a whole lot of polling.

You know how the Eskimos have fifty different words

***The Big Easy* (1987)**

This Cajun-hot film helped put Dennis Quaid on the love map. When Quaid drawls, "Baby, your luck is about to change" before showing Ellen Barkin what's what, the women in the audience summarily moan.

***The Last Seduction* (1994)**

A sexy film noir starring Linda Fiorentino, a coke dealer who turns fugitive after absconding with her hubby's money. There are a few steamy trysts with *Chicago Hope* actor Peter Berg, who plays the besotted hick who falls for the femme fatale. The woman is definitely in the driver's seat here.

***9 ½ Weeks* (1986)**

Striptease, food and a little mainstream B&D (bondage and discipline) in this sexual porridge featuring that freaky Mickey Rourke and the beautiful Kim Basinger.

***Bound* (1996)**

Erotic lesbian sex combined with a murder mystery, starring the quirky Jennifer Tilly and lithe Gina Gershon.

***Two Girls and a Guy* (1998)**

The movie is not so great, but the sex scene with Robert Downey Jr. is a winner.

for snow? Masturbation is such an important part of a man's life that men have invented fifty different ways of describing the act (jerking off, whacking off, choking the weasel, spanking the monkey, wanking, pulling the pud, slapping the meat, beating off, turning Japanese . . .). Well, it's time for you to set up your own bedroom playstation.

While men understand that masturbation is as natural as

peeing (and a lot more fun), women have been taught that there is something shameful about pleasuring themselves. The fact is, masturbation will get you in touch (pun intended) with your sensuality and help you enjoy sex more when you do have a partner.

As sex educator and mistress of masturbation Betty Dodson explains in her book *Sex for One,* "Masturbation is the ongoing love affair that each of us has with ourselves throughout our lifetime. . . . It's an opportunity for us to explore our bodies and minds for all those sexual secrets we've been taught to hide, even from ourselves. We don't have to perform or meet anyone else's standards, to satisfy the needs of a partner, or to fear criticism or rejection for failure."

Men are incredulous to learn that Dodson teaches *seminars* on masturbation for women. To guys, that's like showing someone how to breathe. The fact is, many women are so far removed from their bodies that they actually have to be taught how to have an orgasm!

Don't be embarrassed if you've never masturbated or if you are not sure whether you've had an orgasm. You are not alone. But you are missing out on a whole heap of pleasure, so listen up to what I'm about to tell you.

The song says that diamonds are a girl's best friend, but savvy women know that it's a vibrator that no woman should be without. You can buy one at your local GNC (the Hitachi Magic Wand, which doubles as a back massager, is considered one of the best and costs about $40), or you can order one from a department store catalog.

If you're too shy to go to a sex shop, Good Vibrations in San Francisco (800-289-8423) and Eve's Garden in New York (800-848-3837) offer a whole range of styles and prices. You don't have to get a disembodied penis if you don't want to, but some women prefer vibrators that can be inserted.

You can even get attachments that will give you and

your partner (if you have one) more stimulation. Experiment with the speed, intensity and position that feel good to you. I promise you that these battery-operated sex toys will keep you coming, and coming and coming.

Men Like Pornography

This is a hot-button issue for so many women who find pornography degrading and a precursor to rape. Understand that I'm not endorsing snuff (supposedly featuring real-life torture and murder), kiddie or exploitative films. That kind of porn is sick and illegal.

I'm talking about mainstream porn, the kind you see on the Playboy Channel, in *Penthouse* or in your local video store. *The Texas Chainsaw Massacre* is offensive. Blowing people's heads off is obscene. Blowing a few men on film is not—at least to me.

The fact is, pornography is one of the best ways to learn about men and sex. As homework, read the letters in *Penthouse* magazine to learn about what excites men. (Read them out loud to your boyfriend and see what happens.)

No matter what the editors claim, these letters are about as real as the centerfold's breasts. They may be based on real letters sent in by readers, but they are professionally written by underpaid editorial assistants. That's okay; it's part of the fantasy to pretend that they are true.

Likewise, porn stars are the Academy Award winners of the sex industry. If you want to know how to fake an orgasm, watch the women in a porn flick. You want to know how to give good head, watch a porn star after the director calls, "Action!" You want to learn a variety of positions . . .

The titles of pornos, which are usually puns or takeoffs of mainstream films, will tell you a bit about what is on the sexual menu (e.g., *Black to the Future*, *Cum Rain or Cum*

Shine, My Bare Lady, Behind You All The Way). There is usually little or no plot, the background music is cheesy and the quality of the film and acting is secondary to the sexual gymnastics. The men are all generously endowed, but their shirts are often open to the navel, and they're so sleazy they could slide off a barstool.

If you've never seen a porn film before, you might want to start with one directed by Candida Royale, a former porn star turned auteur. She is the founder of Femme Productions, which makes porn videos with a woman's tastes in mind. There is an actual storyline, more foreplay, better-looking leading men and no close-ups of commingling genitalia. After that, you may want to graduate to the harder stuff, because your boyfriend will be bored and want to fast-forward to the sex scenes.

If you can't decide what to rent, pick one tape for you and one for him. Fair is fair. Make sure you see your film first, because you might not make it to your video if you don't.

Men Like Lingerie

There's a reason why the Victoria's Secret catalog is read by as many men as women: men like lingerie. The problem is, women often wear it in the beginning of the relationship when things are still red-hot, and gradually evolve to *Little House on the Prairie* flannel.

I don't care what you look like or how big you are, you have to incorporate lingerie into your wardrobe. When I first met my boyfriend, I made sure to wear a short skirt with stockings and a garter belt. When I sat down, he could get a peak at what was underneath. Men love that stuff!

As whacked as *The Total Woman* book was in the seventies (the author recommended wrapping your naked self in cellophane and jumping on your man when he came in the door), she had a good point. Every relationship needs variety and an element of surprise to keep it fresh and exciting. When it comes to sex, the ends justify the means. If you want to keep your sex life sizzling, drape yourself in teddies, garter belts, crotchless panties, push-up bras and silk camisoles. If you want to go more RuPaul, shop in the Frederick's of Hollywood catalog. Try wearing your lingerie with high heels, because men love women in stilettos.

The point of lingerie is not just how it makes you look, but how it makes you feel. The sexier you feel, the more sensual you will be in bed. Make it a point to surprise your boyfriend with a new flimsy thing each month. Ask him what colors he likes best (black and red are the staples), but always wear what looks best on you.

Men Like Fantasy

Aside from the ménage à trois, men who seek professional sexual services often request a little role-playing. The reason they go to a pro is because they are afraid that their wives or girlfriends will ridicule their fantasies.

The most common male fantasies involve sex with strangers (often the lusty next-door neighbor), watching others have sex, two women together, light bondage (either being tied up or tying a woman up), spanking (either giving or receiving) and an array of female characters from cheerleaders, coeds and secretaries to nurses, teachers and French maids.

You can explore these fantasies by visiting a nearby theatrical costume or sex shop. You can also instantly transform yourself into a stranger by getting a variety of wigs in different lengths and hair colors. I know this all sounds like a lot of work, but I'm just the messenger here. Besides, the upside to pretending to be a hooker is having him actually *pay* you for your services (it's gotta be real, right?). Go out and buy yourself something nice afterward.

Men Like to Talk Dirty

For most men, phone and cybersex are the next best thing to being there. I know I said that men are visual, but they are also aural. When they hear or read something sexy, pictures spring up in their minds, and the next thing you know, they're reaching out and touching someone. It's safe, and there are no dirty sheets to launder afterward.

First it was phone sex, with 900 numbers burning up the phone wires and credit cards maxing out at $1 per minute. Now we have cybersex, which is less expensive and equally interactive. Honey, why not use our God-given technology for the greater good of our sex lives?

If you're the kind of woman who blushes at the word *vagina,* this may not be for you. But the more naughty words you use, the easier it gets. I know that dirty talking does not sound sexy to women. We prefer polite, sweet-sounding words like *love, tickle, kiss, please* and *thank you.*

Men prefer *pussy, cock, ass, tits, clit, fuck, suck, harder* and *faster.* Like any new language, you can learn to talk dirty by using these words in a sentence. Typically, men refer to a woman's vulva as *beaver* (first appeared in print in 1927), *box* (dates back to Shakespeare's time), *clam* or *bearded clam, hair pie, hole, muff, poontang/tang, quim, slash, snatch* or *trim.* The butt is commonly called *booty, piece of ass, tail* or *back.*

You can practice talking dirty by calling your boyfriend and teasing him with a few sexy suggestions. You can also e-mail him a risqué message (be careful not to send it to him at work, because e-mails are often the property of the company, and you don't want to read your message in the next company newsletter).

Meet in a private chat room and have cybersex. Then recreate what you just said or wrote in real life. Go ahead, try it. He might even say please *and* thank you.

Men Like Women Who Bring on the Noise

Women love to talk, but for some reason when we get in bed we suddenly get real quiet. In addition to talking dirty, men want to know that you're enjoying yourself. They can't read your mind, and they don't really care enough to ask.

So tell them, if not in words, then by your moans, groans and screams for more! It doesn't hurt to arch your back or thrash around like a fish out of water, either.

Men Like Women Who Are Flexible

One of the secrets of a successful sex life is flexibility in both your mind and body. Let's take the body first. The more limber you are, the more positions you can get into. Yoga and stretching will definitely improve your flexibility in bed.

Men in general are not flexible creatures. Few can do splits, and many can't even touch their toes. But when it comes to sex, they don't have to be contortionists. They need arm and leg strength, and it helps if they can bench-press your body weight.

You, on the other hand (or foot), are. If you look at the erotic positions of the *Kama Sutra,* you will see that there are many more than two positions. Try them out for fun. You can always go back to your old faithfuls.

Men Like Quickies

I know that women dream of deep, wet kisses that last for days and long, sweaty nights of lovin' where the foreplay is slow, sweet and forever. Men like this, too, but they are just as happy (if not happier) with a wham-bam quickie. That's why they like McDonald's as much as they like a filet mignon. It's fast, fun and efficient.

Girlfriend, learn to love the quickie. Sometimes it's absolutely fabulous to be taken without dropping a stitch of clothing. Quickies are like between-meal snacks. They are bridges that keep you sated until the next meal. And let's face it, if your man is older, a quickie may be all you get. Young men, God love them, have stamina, but the older a man gets, the faster he is on the draw.

Men Like Lesbians

Anyone who has ever listened to Howard Stern knows that men like to watch two women having sex with each other. Not the lavender flag-waving, duck-tailed lesbians, of course. Men enjoy watching women have sex as long as (a) the women are traditionally beautiful, with long hair, large breasts and lithe bodies; and (b) the women are really interested in the man who is watching and waiting for his turn to jump in and finish the job.

This is such a major fantasy for men that many stroke magazines feature a pictorial of two women in every issue. This is also why topless clubs have sideshows where two thong-clad dancers wrestle in shaving cream or mud, usually in a boxing ring. (To be fair, women get to enjoy a similar show every time they see a team of burly boys tackling each other on the football field.)

The woman-on-woman fantasy is harmless, so don't be alarmed if your boyfriend is so inclined. If he prefers watching two men together or wearing your bra and panties, there is reason for concern.

Men Don't Like Condoms

If you've followed my advice, you're waiting until you've both been tested more than once before having sex. However, I'm realistic enough to know that not everyone is going to follow my sage advice. In that case, you must use a condom whenever you are having sex.

We've all heard the analogy about taking a shower with a raincoat. And nothing stops a moment cold like riffling through your purse or dresser for that little foil package. Well, tough nuggies. Like it or not, dating and condoms will go together as long as you can get pregnant, sick or dead from having sex.

Men may not like condoms, but they wear jock straps to protect their jewels, don't they? Ultimately, girlfriends, it is your responsibility to see to it that he rolls one on before you open your legs. Putting one on him can be part of the foreplay (make sure you leave a half-inch space at the end of the condom to minimize the risk of tearing).

Condoms are much more woman-friendly these days, and some cities have entire stores (Condomania in New York) devoted to this item. Rubbers are available in a variety of brands, colors and flavors. They even come with ridges or tiny bumps that can increase your pleasure during intercourse. One brand glows in the dark, so when he gets excited, you'll feel like you're at a concert begging for an encore.

Make sure that you keep a supply in a cool, dry place within an arm's reach of the bed. All the condoms you buy should be made of latex. Avoid the so-called natural condoms made from sheep or lamb membrane, because they are porous and can allow sexually transmitted viruses to get through.

Always use a water-based spermicide that contains nonoxynol–9, which provides an extra safeguard against HIV infection, the virus that causes AIDS.

Lubricants are okay as long as they are water-based, such as K-Y jelly, or prelubricated with spermicidal foam or gel. Never use petroleum jelly, baby oil, cold cream or shortening because oil-based lubricants can weaken latex condoms, causing them to break or tear. Go to the drugstore before you get hot and heavy.

If a man says no to a condom, you say no to him. End of story. If he says, "You don't trust me," tell him it's not a matter of trust, it's a matter of health—yours and his. If he says, "I'm clean," tell him, "That's great, but I want to use a condom anyway." If he says, "I'll lose my erection," tell him you'll help him get it back.

Men Don't Like Kissing

I don't know why this is, but long, deep kissing (on the mouth) is something that women enjoy much more than men. According to the Kinsey Institute, lesbians are the most enthusiastic smoochers, 95 percent of whom kiss when they make love. Even gay men are less likely to kiss than their female counterparts, weighing in at 71 percent.

This may have something to do with the fact that men are so genital-oriented that they see kissing as more intimate than sucking. Plus, they don't want to even think about kissing you after you have spent some time down south.

What a shame. But some men do love kissing and are quite good at it. It's usually a sign that they are good at other oral activities. And speaking of oral sex, just because men enjoy getting blow jobs doesn't mean they are willing to reciprocate.

Men are often afraid of giving oral sex to women because they don't know where they're going and they hate to ask for directions. Some men are turned off by the smell (said to be fishy), although others are turned on by it.

You can remedy a man's aversion to kissing by letting

him know that it turns you on. Show him what you like by example. If he still turns up his nose at the idea, you might have to move on to another sex partner, depending on how important these activities are to you. Men don't stay with women who don't satisfy them sexually—why should you?

Men Like Compliments

Women are used to being ogled at, cat-called and told they're sexy. Men, on the other hand, rarely get the same treatment. As a result, they love it when they get the rare compliment from a woman.

Notice the areas on your boyfriend's body that you admire, and tell him that you love his muscular legs, handsome face, strong hands, whatever. Compare him to a leading man in the movies, and watch him puff up the next time he passes a mirror.

Most of all, make sure you tell him what he does in bed that drives you insane. Nothing pleases a man more than feeling like he's a stud in bed. Don't tell your girlfriends, tell him! I'm not suggesting that you lie to him if he's subpar. But, like he's Pavlov's dog, reward him for a job well done.

Men Like to Bring Home the Trophy

Men like to bring home the trophy; why shouldn't you? You're in love, the sex is great and you're starting to think till death do you part. But before you bring home the man of your dreams, review the following checklist:

- You live in the same general region.
- You have similar educational backgrounds.

- You both want or don't want children.
- Your parents are both divorced or are both still together.
- You are equally attracted to each other.
- You trust each other.
- You have similar attitudes about sex.
- You have similar views about money.
- You have similar views about politics.
- You have similar views about drugs and alcohol.
- You are both gainfully employed.
- You make each other laugh.
- You'd rather be with each other than with anyone else.

Okay, but you're still not quite ready yet. Just a few more things before you wear the rings:

Volunteer Together

Try being a Big Brother and Big Sister to a needy child. You'll see how he interacts with kids, and you'll get to play together as well. Visiting a nursing home will also give you insight into how he feels about the elderly.

Cook Together

This can be fun, à la *Annie Hall* and the lobsters, but it can also backfire if you're the kind of cook who is temperamental in the kitchen.

Go to the Supermarket Together

You can find out a lot about a person by the way he shops. Does he make a beeline for the beer and chips or for the gourmet food section? Food compatibility is important for many couples.

Take a Vacation Together

If you can endure the stress of airport baggage claims, hours of driving, shared bathrooms and just plain being together nonstop for a week or two, you will probably make it as a couple. If his personality changes as soon as he crosses the town border, you need to know that side of him as well. Plus, it's a great way to test your sexual compatibility.

Once you've decided to share body and soul with him, it's time to close the deal. Unfortunately, this is when most women make their biggest mistakes. Here are a few more questions to ask yourself to see if your relationship will go the distance:

CAN YOU TRUST HIM?

Trust is essential in any relationship. Does he keep his word—when he says he's going to do something, does he do it? Does he show up when and where he says he will? Does he make you feel safe?

DOES HE HAVE A BAD TEMPER?

The best way to determine if a guy has a violent temper is to watch how he behaves while driving. Does he cut people off? Give another driver the finger? Roll down the window and curse? Honk incessantly? Has he ever pulled over and physically threatened a motorist? These are all signs that he may have an anger problem.

If you live in a city, go for a cab ride with him and see how he reacts. Or watch what he does when he's ignored by a waiter. How does he react when someone accidentally bumps into him on the street? Same test, different circumstances.

IS HE A PLAYER?

Unless he's a misogynist, you shouldn't have a problem *dating* a player. You're a player, too! You want someone who is out there having as much fun as you are and who won't resent you for having more than one man in your life. However, some players want to play forever.

Players who want to stay players are not marriage material. If he still wants his freedom after a year of dating, let the man go! Tell him straight out: "I'm looking for a more permanent relationship right now. If you're not interested in being exclusive, I understand, but I'm going to move on." If he really wants to be with you, he'll be more than willing to stop dating.

IS HE WILLING TO GO OUT OF HIS WAY FOR YOU?

Make a request to see how much he cares for you. Ask him if he'll pick you up or take you to the airport. That's a biggie! If he really likes you, he'll brave the traffic and parking nightmare.

DOES HE HAVE THE DRIVE TO SUCCEED IN THE WORLD?

This is not so much about money as it is about having goals for the future. Men without ambition will want you to support them in the future.

WILL HE GO TO A WEDDING OR FUNERAL WITH YOU?

If the man you've been dating for a while is willing to go with you to a major event like a wedding or funeral, you are officially a couple. If he's able to interact well with your family and friends during these emotionally stressful gatherings and he passes all your other tests, he's the one!

IS HE WILLING TO INVEST IN YOU?

When a man is serious about a woman, he will start investing money in her. If he starts buying you expensive gifts like a car or a computer, he's thinking about the future. If he offers to help you with a down payment on a house or apartment, he probably wants to share it with you. No man is going to part with that much money if he doesn't intend to stick around.

HAS HE INTRODUCED YOU TO HIS BOSS AND WORKMATES?

For many men, meeting the boss and workmates is almost as important as meeting his family. A man would never introduce a woman he isn't serious about to his boss, because he knows that the girlfriend he chooses says a lot about who he is. Taking you to a company function is the male equivalent to bringing you to a wedding.

HAVE YOU DISCUSSED THE FUTURE?

Have you noticed a change in pronouns during your conversations from "I" to "we"? Have you gone house hunting together to scout for your dream place? Have you talked about where you would both like to go on your honeymoon? These kinds of discussions signal the last lap of your dating career. The checkered flag is down, and you're so close to a proposal you can almost taste it.

Men Know Marriages Are Like Mergers and Acquisitions

Before you say "I do" to any man, you might want to do a some digging to make sure that you're not making a serious mistake. I know this seems harsh, but look at your potential relationship like it's a merger and acquisition. If a man's in the M&A biz, he is responsible for bringing two companies together whose assets will benefit each other and make them one strong corporation.

Do you think he goes on gut instinct alone? Not when there's big money involved. Those who specialize in mergers and acquisitions investigate both companies, do financial background checks, interview the officers, and evaluate the annual reports. They know everything there is to know and more before the deal is struck. What's more important than your personal lifetime merger?

I know a matchmaker here in New York who specializes in bringing high-quality people together. The first thing she does before taking on a client is ask for a blood test. After that, she hires a private investigator to do a complete check. This is part of her service. She finds that people aren't always who they say they are.

A guy may seem perfectly together, well dressed, polite, fun-loving and happy, when he's really going home to a bottle of vodka or a refrigerator full of human heads. You never know.

Some women hire ex-cops to do the gumshoe work.

The bottom line is, no birth control is 100 percent. If you sleep with a man, there is always the possibility that you will become pregnant. Does this man have the financial wherewithal to support a family? Is he the kind of man you want your baby to have as a father? These are crucial life issues.

I'm not saying you have to hire a PI to have him tailed, but you can do a background check. Find out if he's ever been arrested or whether he has some ex-wives he hasn't told you about. Invite him to do the same thing to you. That's only fair. Marriage is serious business. If he is horrified by the idea, perhaps he has something to hide. Better to find out now rather than to pay the price of a bad decision years down the road, especially if there are children involved.

Men Want to Be the One to Propose

If you are following this program, you will have no trouble finding a man who wants to marry you. But some men need a little push, especially those who required you to use all of your flirting skills to ask you out on a date.

Don't ask him to marry you, because a man will always want this to be his decision. But if he hasn't popped the question after a few years of dating, and you know that he is the man you want to spend the rest of your natural-born days with, it's time to sit down and have an engagement summit.

Never schedule the summit on one of the male or female holidays, or when he's stressed out after a long day at work. Pick a relaxing time to tell him you want to find out if you are on the same page as far as your relationship is concerned. Tell him (even if you don't believe it) that it's all right if he's not ready, but you need to know when he will be so you can start making your own plans for the future.

Give him up to three months to make a decision; no extensions. Men can come up with a thousand excuses about why you should wait. "I want to wait until we can afford a nice honeymoon." (Tell him you're willing to put off the honeymoon until you've saved some money.) "My mother is very ill and a wedding will cause her too much stress." (Tell him you want her to be around to see you married.) "My family doesn't approve of our relationship." (Okay, you'll elope.)

If he's not interested, it's time to make room for someone who is. Sometimes the summit is enough to propel him into action. But you must be willing to walk away; otherwise he'll know that you are willing to keep things as they are forever.

Men Have Different Proposal Styles

For a woman, the way a man proposes is almost as important as her wedding day. Women are romance freaks. We still want our boyfriends to ask our parents for our hand in marriage and to get down on one knee with a ring in the back pocket. Now for the reality check: maybe that'll happen, and maybe it won't. Baby, it doesn't matter how he proposes as long as asks you!

Some men will go as far as hiring a plane to write "Will you marry me" in the sky. Others want to do it in a restaurant over champagne and dessert. Some are willing to do it on national television.

Try not to get caught up in your romantic ideals. How your man proposes to you is not as important as the fact that he is asking in the first place. If the proposal lacks in romance, make up for it on the honeymoon.

PART VI

Achieving Your Personal Best With or Without a Man

Ever wonder why the word *bachelor* has such a positive ring to it? The reason is that men know being single can be fun. Even though your ultimate goal is to find someone to share your life with, there will be times in your dating career when you will be alone.

Learning how to live large when you are by yourself might be the most important chapter of this book, because it will show you that being single doesn't necessarily mean being lonely. I know it's hard, but you should use this time to do the inner work. Exchange those negative thoughts and feelings of longing for a more positive attitude about being single.

Remember the exercise where you smile at yourself in the mirror? It probably felt fake at first, but if you practice long enough, smiling will become second nature. The same idea holds true for thoughts.

Psychologists have found that optimists not only live longer than pessimists do, but are healthier, too. Optimists recover faster from illnesses and have more friends ('cause, honey, who wants to hang out with a complainer?). Some people have a brighter outlook by nature, but optimism can also be learned.

Repeat the following thoughts to yourself every morning before you get out of bed, and every night before you go to sleep:

- I enjoy being single.
- I have a full life.
- I have great friends who are loving and supportive.
- I'm going to find a man soon, but until then I'm doing just fine.
- I don't need to be with a man in order to be happy.
- I'm not putting my life on hold until I find a man; I'm going to do things that I enjoy *now*.

- I may be single, but at least I'm not married and miserable like so many of the couples I know.

If any of the above statements aren't true, *make* them true for you. How? Get up off of that thang, and make yourself feel better. Here are a few ideas:

Develop an Appreciation for Another Kind of Music

Not only will this expand your horizons, it will probably introduce you to a whole new culture and group of people. If you've been a rocker all your life, get dressed up and go to the opera. Learn how to two-step, hip-hop, salsa or swing. Exception: If you can't follow the beat, do yourself a favor and stay off the dance floor.

Join a Book Group

Discuss books and novels with other bibliophiles. Look for a coed book group at your local bookstore or library, or put an ad in the paper and start your own. Stay away from all-women groups that get weepy over *The Bridges of Madison County*.

Redecorate Your House or Apartment

It's all in the theme of out with the old, in with the new. Remember what I said about too many frills and knick-knacks?

Volunteer

Become a tutor and teach someone how to read. Join a group that renovates houses for the needy (a great way to meet men). Work at a soup kitchen. Helping someone will take your mind off of your own sorry self while making you feel good about doing good. It certainly puts being single into perspective.

Write a Romance Novel

Write about your fantasy relationship and set it in any era you choose! Writing a romance novel will unleash that dormant sex goddess within you. It will also prime you for the real thing (as long as you don't expect your new boyfriend to be the son of an oil dynasty named Payton).

Investigate Your Family Tree

Aside from learning about your roots, you might get closer to some relatives you didn't even know you had. Doing a family tree can be an extremely powerful experience. Of course, if your family is so crazy or dysfunctional that the tree looks more like a moth-eaten shrub, ignore this suggestion.

Make a Wedding Quilt

I have a friend who started making her wedding quilt while she was still single. She was absolutely clear about the kind of man she was looking for, and she gave herself a year to finish it. She put a lot of love and energy into her quilt. Within eight months, she met the man she eventually married. This is for the Martha Stewart wanna-bes. I'm lucky if I can sew on a button.

Learn a New Language

French, Italian and Spanish are the Romance languages. After you feel comfortable, visit a country that enables you to immerse yourself in a foreign culture (and its men) to try out your new skills. Nothing is better for the ego than a trip to Europe as a single American woman. If you hate being verbally worshiped by men, stay home. For information on overseas language classes, call Eurocentres at 800-648-4809.

Get a Job You Love

If you don't already have one, of course (it's a great distracter from a slow love life). Changing professions may require going back to school, which is another great way to meet new people.

Get Your Finances in Order

Honey, don't wait for a man to rescue you from your debts. Start planning for your financial future now. Hire a financial advisor to help you invest or play the market. Men love to talk about money, so remember to ask every man you meet for his advice.

Plan a Fabulous Vacation

Looking for an outdoors type of man? Take an adventure trip. Go on a safari or tour the Amazon. Go whitewater rafting, mountain biking, skiing in the Alps or parasailing in Mexico (see my monthly calendar of events). The more exhilarating, the better. You will not only meet more men on these trips, but you'll also have great stories to tell on your dates.

Dine in Fine Restaurants

You don't need a man to take you out in order to enjoy fine dining! Take a foodie friend and treat yourselves to some great meals. You don't have to cook, clean up afterward or eat on a swivel stool in some greasy spoon just because you're single. I recommend Italian restaurants, where the waiters pamper single women. There are also gourmet dining groups that cater to singles.

Join a Wine-Tasting Group

Do you like sophisticated men? If you live in or near a major city, there is probably a restaurant that offers wine-tasting classes. If not, the Learning Annex in New York City sometimes offers these seminars.

The International Wine Center in New York sponsors a three-day beginner wine-tasting course for $145. If you long to clink glasses with budding connoisseurs, call 212-268-7517.

Read a Book in a Public Place

When I was single, I used the book method for years to start up conversations with men in cafés, sports bars, parks and airport lounges. This technique never fails!

Say you're a man, alone and bored, sitting in a restaurant somewhere. You see an attractive woman completely absorbed in a book, oblivious to what's going on around her. You wonder what's captured her interest. The curiosity is driving you crazy, so you get up the nerve to go over to her and ask her what she's reading. Listen, darlin', I've had men leave their dates to talk to me about what I'm reading. Of course, you must read something that a man would be interested in talking about. *Waiting to Exhale* by Terry McMillan is a great novel, but not one that a man would feel comfortable talking about.

I had great luck with books about sports figures such as Muhammad Ali, Mickey Mantle, Michael Jordan, Mario Andretti, Vince Lombardi, Joe DiMaggio, Willie Mays, Babe

Ruth and Gale Sayers. (You might even find them inspirational.) Motivational books by Tony Robbins also work, because men can apply his teachings to their professional lives. Another favorite *is Think and Grow Rich* by Napoleon Hill and *Smart Money* by Tyler Hicks.

When you're asked about what you're reading, close your book, look him in the eye and say, "If you buy me a cup of coffee, I'll give you a synopsis."

In the beginning you may find it difficult to concentrate in a public place. With practice, you can learn to block out the background noise. Give it a try. Your English lit teachers would be so proud.

Start a "Pair and a Spare" Singles Group

If there isn't a PAAS group in your hometown, start one up. All you need to bring are up to three single male friends. You can hold a meeting in your home or local pizza joint.

Take Flying Lessons

I've always wanted to learn how to fly, and pilots are still mostly men. What could be more exhilarating?

Take a Walk with Man's Best Friend

The hottest pickup place in every city is your neighborhood park or doggy run. Dogs break down the shyness barrier and are instant conversation-starters. Never buy a dog just to meet a man, however. You must be an animal lover and be willing and able to care for your four-legged friend.

If you don't have the time or money to care for a pooch, offer to walk a friend's dog on the weekend, or join the Humane Society's volunteer dog-walking program. For more information, call your local animal shelter.

Make Your Own Brews

Most hops shops now offer free introductory and advanced courses on how to brew your own beer. The majority of these classes are 95 percent single men. If you're a brew babe, this is the place for you. This pastime attracts everyone from college students and construction workers to lawyers. Call the American Home Brewers' Association (303-447-0816), or check your yellow pages under Beer or Home Brewing. Aficionados also recommend signing up for beer tastings.

Go to a Bookstore

Nowadays, bookstores like Barnes and Noble are a cross between a library and a café. Many actually have cafés where you can wile away the hours reading and people-watching. They provide myriad opportunities for meeting men, especially if you are browsing in the right sections. Go to the business, computer and sports sections (after you visit the relationship area, of course).

Go to a Library

While public libraries tend to attract the elderly and homeless, law, music and medical libraries attract students and professionals. If there isn't one in your hometown, go to the nearest city, university or college.

Avoid Street Fairs and Flea Markets

Most single men would rather sit through a chick flick than go to a street fair or flea market, so don't bother going unless you like being outside and eating until you feel nauseous. Look at the agonized faces of the married men pushing strollers if you don't believe me.

Parks

Parks are like outdoor bookstores and gyms. You can sit, read, play sports and people-watch. Go to the basketball courts or softball fields if you want to meet guys, or strap on some in-line skates (and protective gear) and take off.

Readings and Lectures

Like most adult education courses, these are better places to meet other women than men. You will find the occasional bookish man, but chances are the boys are in the park, gym or sports bar. That doesn't mean you shouldn't go if you are interested in the subject. But the truth is, honey, women want intellectual stimulation, men want physical stimulation.

Geography Is Destiny

Girlfriends, when it comes to men, geography can be destiny. The following are the top twenty cities with the highest percentage of men between eighteen and thirty-four (the primary dating years) as of 1998, according to *Single Living* magazine.

1. Anchorage, AL
2. Billings, MT
3. Denver, CO
4. Las Vegas, NV
5. Norfolk, VA
6. Phoenix/Scottsdale, AZ
7. San Francisco, CA
8. San Diego, CA
9. Seattle, WA
10. Washington, D.C.
11. Houston, TX
12. New Orleans, LA
13. Ft. Lauderdale, FL
14. Miami, FL
15. San Jose, CA
16. Atlanta GA
17. Eugene, OR
18. Cleveland, OH
19. Burlington, VT

Walking Tours

This is a great activity if you are on the gray side of forty. The best way to meet a potential partner is to join a regular walking tour group rather than one that caters to tourists and other transients.

Get Religion

The oldest and probably the best way to meet serious-minded, morally conscious men. Most churches, temples and mosques have activities for single and divorced folk such as dances, dinners, trips, lectures and seminars. If your church or synagogue doesn't have a singles group, start one. You may find more than God. But you have to go regularly in order to get the spiritual and social benefits, however.

Drink Coffee

Starbucks and other coffee chains are the mecca for thousands of hyped-up singles all across the country. Here's what I tell my clients to do whenever they are in a café:

If you see a man you are interested in sitting at another table, ask the waiter to deliver a note saying: "Hi, I see you're sitting alone. If you'd like to join me for a cappuccino, please feel free to come over."

If he's sitting at a counter or table with an empty chair, sit down next to him. You can say, "Excuse me, I've never eaten here before. I was wondering if you could recommend something?"

Another great trick is to pretend that all the other chairs have been taken and ask if he would mind sharing his table. If he invites you to sit down, start a pleasant conversation and let the fates take it from there.

Commute

If you're single and commute to work by train, chances are you've spotted that rare good-looking guy *without* a wedding band buried in his newspaper. Most people are creatures of habit, so start by sitting in the same seat every day. After a while, you can nod a greeting in the morning. If he doesn't initiate a conversation, ask him if you can read a section of his paper when he's through. Before you know it, you'll be commuter pals. If you prefer driving to work, find out about the car pools in your neighborhood and ride share.

Men Love Sports (Duh!)

Men love sports. So why not go directly to the source to recruit some athletic boys? Sure, you can go to your book clubs and aerobics classes, but you're not gonna find much testosterone there.

Look in the locker room, girl! Pack your gym bag, get off your butt and get moving. You must choose your sport carefully, however. Make sure the activity matches your personality and that of the type of guy you're looking for:

Coed Softball

Baseball fans are fun-loving lads. The game also attracts intellectuals. Check to see if your company has a coed team. If not, start one.

Martial Arts

Karate and other martial arts are filled with men who are both physically and spiritually inclined.

Surfing

Great if you like blonds, valley boys and free spirits. More brawn than brains here.

Skiing

A sport for the financially well-endowed. A great place to find boys with healthy trust funds. Look for corporate moguls doing the moguls.

Biathlons

Great for Type A women looking for their counterparts. A good place to meet company men proving their mettle.

Biking

Mountain bikers are competitive and high achievers. Biking clubs usually meet on the weekends and they are a fun, regular activity. In the winter, you can spin if you belong to a gym.

Sailing

Another patrician sport. Great if you're looking for Republicans and politically conservative men.

Rock Climbing

Guys who climb are high achievers. They're always reaching for the top. This sport is more about mental strength than physical strength, but the male–female ratio is six to one. With numbers like this, girlfriend, it is worth risking a few cuts and scrapes. Courses starting at the beginner's level are offered at most health clubs. To find one in your area, check with a local sports equipment store.

Running

These men usually go the distance in relationships. They're dependable and focused, but a little obsessive. If you're interested in losing weight, for example, join your local Road Runners Club. I'm currently enrolled in a marathon program because I plan to run the New York Marathon this year. More than half the members are men. Why not lose weight and meet men at the same time? And not just any man: a goal-oriented, health-conscious man.

Scuba Diving

Baby, these guys are deep. They like to explore and are usually great conversationalists.

River Rafting

Are you adventurous? Do you like taking risks? Guys who raft are able to weather the rough patches in a relationship.

Golfing

This used to be an elitist sport, but now that everyone's doing it, some of the snob appeal has gone. Take up golfing if you want steady, dependable men. Unfortunately, many of these men are already married. Plus, you have to be invited or extremely wealthy in order to join the nicest golf clubs. There are public courses, however, with no restrictions.

Yoga

If you like educated, environmental types who wear Birkenstocks and eat granola, this is the sport for you. Yoga is extremely trendy right now, thanks to Madonna and "power" yoga, which requires strength as well as flexibility. Guys who are into yoga are usually spiritual and low-key. You won't find many stockbrokers sitting cross-legged and chanting oooooommmmmmm.

Clay Shooting

Shooting ranges are frequented by frustrated hunters trying to perfect their shots between seasons. Men and women come together to exchange helpful hints between stations, and if you don't meet someone on the course, you've got another opportunity at the clubhouse. Clay shooters tend to be macho but humble, because they have to be able to take it when they miss their shots (and they do miss a lot).

Most ranges provide lessons and the necessary equipment. For more information call Black's Wing and Clay, 800-224-9464, which provides a state-by-state list of courses.

Weightlifting

Let's face it, honey, boys don't take classes at the gym unless it's boxing, spinning or weight training. Investigate a few fitness clubs (YMCAs provide a less expensive route), or join a nearby club and start to pump some iron. Ask one of the buff dudes to spot for you while you lift a barbell, or to show you how to adjust your spinning bike.

You will also find the boys on the treadmills and stationary bikes, so position yourself next to a cutie, and don't change the TV channel from the game to *Felicity*. In fact, if he's watching a game while running, ask him what the score is to break the ice.

Men Like Golf Courses, Not Continuing Ed

Ever wonder why most of the people you see taking seminars and adult education classes are women? Because men don't take courses unless they help them with their careers. A man's identity is connected to his job and how much money he makes, in the same way a woman's identity (at least those women who haven't read this book) is connected to her relationships and physical appearance. This is why it is essential that you think like a man when you select the courses you take. Here are a few suggestions:

Computer programming
Managing your portfolio
How to be a better manager
How to pay less taxes
Playing the market
Internet investments
Improving your memory
Get rich in real estate
How to live to be 100

If you must take something artistic (i.e., interesting) and you are willing to travel and sift through the gay men, the following courses will get your creative juices flowing.

Acting/Filmmaking

Looking for your leading man? The International Film and Television Workshop in Rockport, Maine, offers one-week courses that start at $500. Call 207-236-8581.

Creative Writing

Hone your writing skills at the Summer Writing Festival at the University of Iowa in Iowa City. Weekend workshops start at $150. Call 319-335-2534.

Painting

Maybe the sexy guy with the paint-smudged jeans will sit as your model. Chicago's Arrowmont School offers one-week drawing and painting courses that will only run you about $300. Call 615-436-5860.

Men Look for Bedmates, Not Soulmates, in Bars

If you're looking for serious-minded men, stay away from the bars and clubs. If you want to find a committed man, go to places where men are committed to doing something. Men in bars are committed to getting drunk and staying single.

Men Shop on a Need-to-Go Basis

For many women, shopping is a passion, a hobby, a pulse-raising thrill ride. For men, shopping is a necessity, like having to go to the bathroom. With this in mind, don't shop for the man of your dreams in the produce section of your local grocery, like so many other dating guides tell you to do. Instead, here's what men like to buy:

Hardware (the male equivalent of cosmetics counters)
Electronics (Radio Shack, Sharper Image, etc.)
CDs (HMV, Tower, Sam Goody, Virgin)

Computers (Comp USA, COMDEX conventions)
Liquor (browse the wine or Scotch sections)
Cars (BMW, Mercedes, Lexus, classics, car shows)
Cameras (video, 35mm, wide and telephoto lenses)
Sporting goods (refer to my sports list for which sections to visit)
Boats (boat shows, marinas)

Men Go Places (A Calendar of Events)

When I told you it's raining men, honey, I meant it's monsoon season all year long! If you haven't found Mr. Right-in-Your-Own-Backyard, why not go on a vacation for a little Mr. Right Away? Here's a month-by-month calendar of places to go where you can soak up some son, ah, I mean sun, and have some fun while you're at it.

JANUARY/FEBRUARY

Take the Plunge

You won't find a bronzed God lazing on the beach. Most straight men hate to sit and sizzle; they like to *do* things. So enroll in a scuba class (local dive shops have basic courses to get you started). Plan a trip to the Virgin Islands or the Florida Keys, where you can practice diving and earn your diving certification. Call the Professional Association of Diving Instructors (800-729-7234) in Santa Ana, California, for a free catalog of certified dive shops around the world.

MARCH

Take a Powder

If you take only one vacation this year, go to Aspen or Vail, Colorado, for a little powdery spring skiing. You've never even ventured down a bunny slope? No problem. Take a one-on-one lesson (instructors tend to be like *Baywatch* babes on skis). Another potential man-meeting spot is the ski lift, which offers 15 minutes of cozy togetherness, and après-ski is the time for relaxed mingling at the lodge. For information, call Aspen Central Reservations at 800-262-7736 or Vail Valley Central Reservations at 800-525-3875.

APRIL

Link Up

Pack up your golf clubs for a fun weekend trip to Hilton Head Island in South Carolina, where there are more than two dozen golf courses! You can show off the golf lessons you've been taking since January. Don't wait to go in the summer, because it will be flooded with families and college kids. In the spring you'll find a lot of businessmen on their office retreats.

Call the Chamber of Commerce (800-523-3373) for more travel information. There are free golf clinics and seminars for ladies only at more than two hundred private and public golf courses every May.

MAY

It's Two-Love

Whether you're a pro or a novice, tennis camp is the perfect getaway to meet men. The John Gardiner Tennis Ranch on Camelback, a singles-friendly spot located in Sedona, Arizona, is your best bet for making a perfect match. The weeklong programs include instruction and tournaments, plus unlimited court time. The ranch also has swimming pools, a fitness room, jogging trails and a spa. For information, call 800-245-2051.

JUNE

Gone Trolling

June can be a tough month for single travelers. Let's face it: The last thing you want is a vacation spot overrun with starry-eyed honeymooners.

It's time to go fly-fishing in Montana, where you'll find hundreds of rugged single men. Fly-fishing outfitters sponsor a variety of trips and accommodations ranging from cabins to luxurious lodges.

Two outfitters to try: Bud Lilly's Fly Fishing School, 39 Madison Avenue, West Yellowstone, MT 59758; 800-854-9559; and the Orvis Fly-Fishing School, Box 798, Manchester, VT 05254 (800-235-9763).

JULY

Go with the Flow

Few adventures put you in touch with the forces of nature the way whitewater rafting does. If you're looking for something wet and wild, go west, young women. One of the most popular and challenging rafting experiences is at the Grand Canyon section of the Colorado River. For information on Colorado River trips, call the Grand Canyon Expeditions Company (800-544-2691).

Eastern rafting outfitters include North American River Runners in Hico, West Virginia (800-950-2585), Natahala Outdoor Center in Bryson City, North Carolina (800-232-7238) and Northern Outdoors in the Kennebec Valley Region of Maine (800-765-7238).

Five hundred outfitters and operators worldwide belong to a trade association called America Outdoors. This org-anization maintains a database of its members at www.americaoutdoors.org.

Singled Outdoors

The National Outdoor Leadership School (NOLS), which is headquartered in Wyoming, offers whitewater rafting, horse-packing and rock-climbing courses in the lower forty-eight states. NOLS discourages couples and families because it wants each participant to interact with the others.

Their trips are not for the faint of heart, however. They stress physical endurance (although there is transportation backup for participants who can't hack it). There are two twenty-day canoe trips on the South Macmillan River in the Yukon Territory during the summer months. For more information contact NOLS, 288 Main Street, Lander, WY 82520, 307-332-5300, www.nols.edu.

AUGUST

Bicycle Built for Two

Take a bike trip past the ocean views and quaint towns of Martha's Vineyard or Nantucket, two gorgeous islands off the coast of Massachusetts. The ratio of men to women might not be as favorable as on a 100-mile-a-day ride, but a short jaunt has its advantages.

These trips offer the same amenities as other organized excursions, including inn accommodations and gourmet meals. And if there's no chemistry on the bike trail, both islands offer a lively nightlife. For information call Bike Rider Tours (800-473-7040).

SEPTEMBER

Ride 'Em, Cowboys

If you're a cowgirl at heart, head to the open range and leave your hair dryer and cell phone behind. Try visiting Breteche Creek, a 7,000-acre working cattle and horse-breeding ranch in Cody, Wyoming. Breteche provides tent cabins and three squares of gourmet eats, as well as meals by the campfire (complete with singing cowboy!).

The range offers horseback riding, cattle rustling, hiking, whitewater rafting, a wood-stoked hot tub and guided tours of Yellowstone National Park.

For off-ranch activities, you must go to Cody Nite Rodeo, followed by some Fat Tire beers at Cassie's Bar across the street. I promise you'll be two-steppin' with a red-meat-eating, Stetson-wearing cowboy in no time.

For more information, contact Breteche Creek Guest Ranch, P.O. Box 596, Cody, WY 82414, 307-587-3844, e-mail breteche@wave.park.wy.us.

OCTOBER

Lots of Fish in the Sea

In the fall, the Outer Banks of North Carolina lure a different sort of beachgoer—saltwater fishermen. The Gulf Stream flows about twenty miles off the Outer Banks, providing some of the Atlantic's richest fishing waters. Charter boats leave year-round from the village of Hatteras.

Hatteras also has one of the few saltwater fishing schools in the country, where you can sign up for a deep-sea excursion or surfcasting course. For information on the Outer Banks, contact the Chamber of Commerce, Box 1757, Kill Devil Hills, NC 27948, 919-441-8144.

NOVEMBER/DECEMBER

Hello, Sailor!

Sign up for an introductory course at the Annapolis Sailing School and plan a trip in the fall or winter to the Gulf of Mexico or the Caribbean. Most sailing schools offer seven-day trips and flotilla cruises. Call 800-638-9192.

From the Mouths of Babes

The best way to find out how to date like a man is to ask the guys themselves. With that in mind, we surveyed 200 New York City men between the ages of twenty-three and forty-five about their dating likes and dislikes.

Not surprisingly, men prefer to be the ones who do the chasing, and they don't mind parting with their money when they're out on a date. But although looks are important, it's not the first quality that a guy seeks in a woman: intelligence, education and personality top the list.

Also, men seem to be willing to date older women and women who have children, though overweight women will not be asked out as much as thinner ones. They especially like it when women have long hair and natural makeup and wear minis with heels.

They don't have a problem with blind dates (the majority would do it again), and they would be flattered if a woman sent a waiter to their table with a drink. Nearly all the guys surveyed said they adore oral sex, and their biggest fantasy involves more than one woman in bed. Read on, girlfriend, to find out what else these boys had to say:

How many women do you date in a month?

More than ten: 57.5%

Five to ten: 19%

Three to five: 10.5%

One to three: 9%

How many different women do you sleep with in a month?

More than ten: 14.5%

Five to ten: 10%

Three to five: 8%

Two to three: 5%

One or two: 62.5%

Should a woman occasionally pay for dinner?

Yes: 25.5%

No: 61.5%

Sometimes: 13%

Would you be flattered if a woman in a restaurant sent you a drink from the bar?

Yes: 92.5%

No: 7%

Do you like women who tell you what to do?

Yes: 29%

No: 51%

Do you like being pursued by a woman?

Yes: 39%

No: 65.5%

Do you like being the one to pursue a woman?

Yes: 89.5%

No: 3.5%

If a woman was overweight but pretty, would you still want to date her?

Yes: 39%

No: 61%

Note: Many of the men also said that intelligence and personality count for a lot.

Are you attracted to women who wear . . . ?

Mini-skirts: 99%
High heels: 100%
Long hair: 95%
Short hair: 1%
Makeup (light and more natural): 28%
No makeup: 44.5%
Lipstick: 39.5%

What does a woman wear that turns you off?

Baggy clothing: 74.5%
Sweat pants: 11%
Spandex: 7.5%

If you could improve anything about yourself, what would it be?

More money: 85.5%
Better body: 6%
More hair: 2%

The characteristics that you want most in a woman in order of importance are:

1. Intelligence/education
2. Personality
3. Looks
4. Body
5. Manners
6. Dance ability
7. Family oriented
8. Sexual history
9. Friends
10. Similar taste in music

Do you watch porn films?

Yes: 55%
No: 39%

Do you like watching porn films alone or with women?

With women: 84.5%
Alone: 39%

Dd you ever stop seing a woman because she refused to have sex with you?

Yes: 9.5%
No: 64%

Have you ever lied about your income to a date?
Yes: 61.5%
No: 28%

Have you ever lied about your occupation to a date?
Yes: 65%
No: 25%

Do you date older women?
Yes: 27.5%
No: 21%

If a woman asked you out on a date, would you call her again?
Yes: 27.5%
No: 50%

Do you ever talk to a woman when you're really interested in her friend?
Yes: 55.5%
No: 44.5%

Does it upset you if you're dating a woman whose refrigerator is always empty?
Yes: 72.5%
No: 24%

How long should you wait before getting married?
A year: 6%
Two years: 55.5%
As long as possible: 28%

Do you like planning your dates?
Yes: 54%
No: 22.5%
Doesn't matter: 16.5%

Does it bother you when a woman orders the most expensive item on the menu?

Yes: 25%

No: 65%

Have you ever gone on a blind date?

Yes: 87%

No: 12%

Would you do it again?

Yes: 78%

No: 21%

Would you date a women who has children?

Yes: 65%

No: 9%

What is your favorite sexual fantasy?

Sex with more than one woman: 94.5%

What is the best thing a woman does in bed?

Blow job: 91.5%

Great kisser: 5%

What is your favorite position?

Me on top: 5%

She on top: 7.5%

Doggie-style: 2%

"69": 78%

Do you like women to wear perfume?

Yes: 6%

No: 55%

Who Are the Celebrity Master Daters?

While celebs have no problem finding people who are eager to bask in a few rays of their spotlight, the astronomical divorce rate among the rich and famous clearly indicates that stars often make star-crossed lovers. With that in mind, check out the following to see which femmes fatales are the Master Daters and which are not.

HEATHER LOCKLEAR

Heather Locklear, the TV actress who recently ended her role as the bitch goddess on Melrose Place, has always known how to date like a man. When Heather met first met bad-boy rocker Tommy Lee, she knew that he had a groupie on each tattooed arm. But Heather won Tommy's heart and affection by simply ignoring him.

Tommy was so smitten by the beautiful blonde, whom he spotted at a backstage party, that he sent a friend over to ask for an introduction. The next day, Tommy called Heather's manager to beg for her phone number. Her manager dutifully relayed the message, which Heather spurned.

"I had called like a million times," Tommy said. "I wanted to send her flowers or invite her to something, anything, just to talk to her." Tommy would have to wait several months for a return call.

Heather moved just as slowly when her current husband, Richie Sambora, made his advances toward her. Richie first popped the question in the summer of 1994, but Heather flatly refused to discuss marriage. Not enough time had passed since her separation from Tommy.

But the persistent Richie continued to ask for her hand every few weeks. Several months later, Heather finally accepted. Today, she is blissfully happy with Richie and their young daughter. Heather proves that good women come to those men who know how to wait.

JULIA ROBERTS

Few actresses have mastered the art of dating like a man better than the jolie Julia Roberts. It has been widely reported that during the sizzling summer of 1991, Julia was engaged to Kiefer Sutherland, whom she dumped three days before their wedding. Apparently Julia had discovered Kiefer's dalliance with a buxom stripper named Amanda "Raven" Rice.

Julia rebounded briefly with Sutherland's ex–best friend, Jason Patric, whom she also ditched after flying off with him to Ireland. She followed these rejections with a string of handsome soon-to-be-exes, including Liam Neeson, Dylan McDermott, Daniel Day-Lewis, Ethan Hawke, Matthew Perry and Lyle Lovett (whom she married and divorced). Now if this ain't dating by numbers, honey, I don't know what is.

OPRAH

Oprah's refusal to marry her longtime love Stedman Graham makes her a Master Dater extraordinaire. She knows that she can be a whole person without being married. She has wealth, inner strength, and so much influence that a mere mention of a book or product can send it sailing off the shelves.

Is Oprah lonely all the way up there on the top? Not a chance! She has someone to share her joys and sorrows with, even if they don't share the same last name. There's no prenuptial agreement to worry about, and no children to see on alternative weekends should the relationship take a dive.

Oprah is free to live her life as she pleases and so, for that matter, is Stedman, who remains important in his own right, not because he's Mr. Winfrey. This kind of no-fuss, no-muss partnership is what men everywhere dream of, but few ever attain.

MADONNA

Not only is Madonna the mother of a love child named Lourdes, she is probably the mother of all Master Daters. Like most men, Madonna understands that one can have sex without love, and she has celebrated myriad sybaritic pleasures in her music, videos and book (aptly titled Sex).

Her boy and girl toys have included actors Warren Beatty and Sean Penn (whom she married and divorced), basketball anomaly Dennis Rodman, comedian Sandra Bernhard, party girl Ingrid Cesares and the father of her child, Carlos Leon.

Madonna doesn't need to justify her love to anyone, but motherhood and her newfound spiritualism have set her on a new path of self-discovery. Nowadays, she is pushing a stroller rather than the envelope, but how much can one woman do? She has already showed us that masturbation is okay, spanking is fun, and lingerie is appropriate for any occasion.

CHER

Although Cher started out dating like a woman (at the tender age of sixteen) by hitching her wagon to the older and savvier Sonny Bono, she gradually evolved into a Master Dater. Cher left Bono for greener and hipper pastures in the form of musicians Greg Allman, Gene Simmons and Richie Sambora. But her most ballyhooed relationship was with the tall, dark and underemployed Rob Camilletti, whom the press persisted in calling Cher's "Bagel Boy" for his stint behind the counter at a bagel shop.

Cher has aged gracefully (thanks to the skillful hands of many surgeons) and by doing so has raised the bar for all women who want the right to stay young at heart forever. Every time we see an ugly, old man with a busty, long-legged blonde on his arm, we can shout, Cher and Cher alike!

BARBRA STREISAND

Like all divas, Barbra is so huge that anyone she dates is destined to walk in her shadow. It is the case for her seemingly storybook marriage to TV actor James Brolin. And you know what? He doesn't give a damn. Women have taken a backseat in marriages to powerful men for centuries. His love for her seems genuine, and they make such a handsome couple.

But before Barbra's prince had come, her dance card read like a cross between the Fortune 500 and People magazine's Sexiest Men Alive. With only one marriage, to actor Elliot Gould, under her belt, her post-divorce dating career included actors Richard Burton, Clint Eastwood, Warren Beatty, Richard Gere, Omar Sharif, Ryan O'Neil, Jon Voight and Don Johnson, anchorman Peter Jennings, tennis pro Andre Agassi, billionaire Richard Baskin (of Baskin Robbins), movie mogul Jon Peters, directors Milos Forman and Peter Weller and Canadian Prime Minister Pierre Trudeau.

Clearly, Barbra was a person who likes people, beautiful people. She is a Master Dater because she has steadfastly refused to be humbled just because she's a woman. Do you think Pavarotti is humble? Is George Lucas humble?

Celebs Who Date Like a Woman

MARLA MAPLES

Marla is the classic old-fashioned dater who is so blinded by fame and fortune that she fails to see the wife and kids who get left behind. In her case, the ends justify the man of considerable means. Donald Trump helped launch her show biz career, and he gave her a child and a nice golden parachute with which to support his newest little Trump. I know it's hard to turn down a ride on a Learjet, but, honey, rich and powerful men get bored so fast, they'll probably have a new girlfriend by the time you deplane.

WHITNEY HOUSTON

She's beautiful, talented and wildly successful. Why would she pick a loser like Bobby Brown? I know that underneath all that glitter and glamour she's just a homegirl from New Jersey, but she needs to find a man who's worthy of her.

He doesn't have to be as rich or as successful as she is. Look at Oprah and Barbra. They found men who worship them, not ask them for bail money every time they throw a chair through a window. Alpha Men are fun to date, and I know they're great in the sack, but never, ever marry a bad boy.

MIA FARROW

Mia Farrow has lived a fascinating life, but she chooses her men unwisely. Although she seemed to truly love and respect Frank Sinatra, there is no way that a young woman can have an equal relationship with a man who is generations older and a cultural icon to boot.

André Previn may not be in the same category, but conductors need to be in control and they are usually temperamental and high-maintenance. By the time she got to Woody Allen, she was back to dating icons, not something the average woman has to contend with.

But the lesson to learn from Mia is, when something doesn't seem right, it probably isn't. Never date a man who (a) doesn't like your kids, (b) likes your kids a little too much, or (c) never wants to take a shower in your apartment. Trust your instincts.

MONICA LEWINSKY

Monica is cited many times in this book because she is the poster child for how not to date. As pretty as she is, her weight problem left her feeling unworthy of a normal relationship (i.e., one that did not involve an older, married man). Her parents' divorce made her a woman in search of a father, not a boyfriend.

The combination created a scandal so great that it nearly unseated the President of the United States. Even if you do set your sights on the most powerful man in the world, he should be the one wooing you, not the other way around.

AFTERWORD
Going for the Gold

I hope this book has inspired you to get out there and start dating a Pair and a Spare. I hope it has taught you to get rid of any bitterness toward men that you might be carrying with you and replace it with a *joie de* dating. (The fictional Bridget Jones is funny, but she's nobody's role model.)

By using the strategies offered in this book—strategies that really work—you will meet and date more men than you've ever dreamed possible! But keep in mind that nothing happens overnight. Over the course of time you will see yourself as more attractive and you will find yourself attracting more men. But you must be persistent. If you've gone on dates that didn't live up to your expectations, or if you're going through a dry spell where you're not attracting anyone, you must maintain a positive attitude. As I've said throughout this book, if you believe that your luck won't change—it won't. Just because you've failed today doesn't mean you're going to fail tomorrow. This may be difficult to believe, but the more failures you have, the closer you are to reaching your goal. Scientists know that experiments involve trial and error. So does dating.

Remember, success is a journey, not a destination. Whenever I have a bad day, I try to stay focused on what my goal is and where I want to be. I think about where I'm going, not just where I am today.

I've been accused of being a Pollyanna, that fictional girl who was a perpetual optimist. Well, I don't see this as a negative trait. More adults should try to recapture that childlike feeling that anything is possible!

Succeeding in dating is about being open to new experiences and allowing yourself to fail as many times as it takes before you succeed. If you're truly ready to meet your soulmate, get ready, you're in for an exciting time ahead.

The first *Star Trek* I ever saw (boys love *Star Trek*) involved Kirk and Spock running down a tunnel to save some planet that was being attacked by aliens. Kirk was suddenly stopped by an invisible force field that Spock was somehow able to penetrate. Kirk yelled, "Spock, why can't I get through?" Spock answered, "You are putting up a wall of anxiety. Just lower that wall and you'll get through."

This is similar to what some of us do to ourselves when we're dating. We put up a wall ("Spock, why can't I find a man?") that prevents others from breaking through. Once you lower that wall of anxiety by telling yourself, "Men want to be with me," you will start letting men into your life.

Becoming a Dating Champion

When I tell you to go for the gold, I'm not just talking about that gold band around your finger. I'm talking about being a dating champion.

The biggest source of unhappiness for single women is the belief that there is someone out there that will fulfill all our needs. This kind of thinking turns us into needy children instead of healthy adults who ask instead if there is anyone who might need us!

Being a dating champion means learning how to love yourself for who you are right now. We should always strive to be better people—that's what doing the inner work is about—but we also must accept our limitations and believe that someday someone else will accept them as well, and love us anyway.

And if you've followed the advice in this book, you have also learned how to find the treasure in others, even if they are not perfect, or even perfect for you. If you're lucky, you'll find a perfect ten (a man who meets your top ten needs), but chances are you'll get a six or seven. That's life. Baby, there's a lot of promise in the word *compromise*.

Being a dating champion is knowing that love comes in many forms. It can come from a girlfriend, a casual male friend, a family member, or a family pet. It's having someone or something that will be there for you in your time of need—even if that time is 3:00 A.M.

If you get only one thing out of this book, I hope it's understanding that the best relationships are built on a foundation of friendship. We often see our friends as people we can spend time with until we meet someone more important. Sweetie, our friends are not fillers, they are sources of love. The more friends you have, the more love you'll discover.

It's Time to Start the Audition

Dating is a little like a casting call for a feature film. A director looking for a man to star in a movie often sees hundreds of actors before choosing the one who is right for the part. Well, guess what? You are the director of your dating career. The more men you see, the easier it will be for you to find your leading man.

And while you're auditioning, never, ever stop learning about men. Study them like you're Jane Goodall on an anthropological expedition. It will help improve your dating and communication skills. Talk to them, listen to them, laugh with them.

Honey, if you wanted to live in France, you'd learn how to speak French, wouldn't you?

Finally, for those of you who have questions after reading *Date Like a Man* and can't make it to one of my seminars, please visit my Web site at www.mymymy.com. As your coach, I want to help you through the program and beyond. And I want to hear about all your matches! If you're not yet wired, you can write:

Myreah
c/o HarperCollins Publishers
10 E. 53rd Street
New York, NY 10022–5299

Good luck, girlfriend, and have fun!

Acknowledgments

I want to thank a few amazing women for their love, support and friendship: Lisa Skriloff of Multicultural Marketing Resources, Inc.; my Fairy Godmother and agent, Linda Konner; my co-writer, midwife and voice, Jodie Gould; my editor, a true visionary, Laureen Rowland, and her former and current assistants, Jodi Anderson and Heather Hayes. Girl power!! Also, one amazing man, my beloved.

—MM

Hugs, kisses and a heartfelt shout-out to:

Agent Linda Konner for her savvy, unflagging enthusiasm and creative input.

Myreah for her unconditional love, positive energy and wisdom.

My One Potata Productions posse, Diane Mancher (Polly) and Jean Anne Rose (Bud). You guys are beyond the best.

Editor Laureen Rowland for her skill and goodwill.

The HarperCollins marketing, sales and art departments for spreading the word.

Single women everywhere who know that dating and desperation are not synonymous.

—JG

Terry Cole Whitaker
Heri Edmonds
Kelsey Collie
Charles Johnson
Calvinn Greene
Clinton Carbon

Russell Barnes
Temithoi Harvin
J. Patrick Walker
Albert Plowdin
Darryl Quinton
David Martin
Darryl "Mandrill" Harris
Kurt Harris
Marcus C. Mundy
Paul Gleason
Michael Spond
Yehuda Hyman
Frank Bayer
Carlos Noble
Harper McKaye
Danny Goldman
Rudy Lowe
Barbara Montgomery
Jon Robert Lenny
Craig Asato
Wendy & Allan Kaplan
Gary Hill
Jerral Stringer
Sadie B. Chisolm
Sandra Bowie
Joyce Mateson
Linda Warton
Lavern Reed
Patty Jacobs
Kimberly Green
Jhelisa Anderson
Jill Randolph
Tracy Goss
Sheila Reid
Sharon D. Pinckney
D. Selena Smith
Alaine A. Chapple
Veronica Hamlett
Yvonne Still
Diane Herro Sanford
Donna Walley
Terri Cole
Carrie Morgan
Lora Weily
David Ender
Donna Benner
Michelle Jaffee
Ellen Baumill
Judy Moy
Darryl Roach
Michael Angel
Brad Deplanch
Joe Drago
Kevin Quinn
Austin Alexander
Chad Briggs
Michael Briggs
Tracey Bernstein
Debra Lee Thorton
Paunita Nichols
Jesse Aragone
Diana Yoon
D.J. Aragone
Ginger Simpson
Schawannah Wright
Robert "Bob" Capps
Jeffrey Latimer
Brian Sheehan
Gabrielle Gaberfello

Paul Scott Adamo
Michael Sherman
Howard Warman
Mark K. Kanewski
Ken Davis
Cliff Love
Cory Naham
Robert L. Turner
Michael Gilman
John Paradise
Bruce Ledde
Michael A. Rosen
Angela Smith
Pinch & Gregg Lee
Rosemarie Terenzio
Bobbi Gabelmann
Laurie Rich
Diane Rappaport
Ricki Lake
Gail Steinberg
Betsy Alexander
Ruth Inniss
Ruth Kennison
Lori Dolney-Levine
Connie Best
Barbara Bevon
Pat Kalmanowitz
Juliet Epstein
Jon Beckerman
Harvey Gold
Billy Staton
Charles Perez
Stewart Krasnof
Ray Nunn
Frank Hagen
Jose Gomez
Ed Connelly
Pat Bullard
Larry Furber
Rabbi Marc Gellman
Msgr. Tom Hartman
Jaye Sarowko
John Downey
David Armour
Trip Brooks
Andrew Scher
Patrick McLaughlin
Teresa Curley
Alyssa Kahn
Joni Cohen-Zlotowitz
Leeza Gibbons
Jill Mulikan-Bates
Joyce Coleman
Diana Lewis
Ronnie Livia
Makiko Ushiyama
Cecilia Loving
Donna Coney Island
Eileen Braum
Michelle Paulas
Liz Lewis
Joanne Bray
Elaine Petrone
Barbara George
Georgianna Mandelos
Hope Hathaway
Paul Ferberhaber
David Rodriguez
Lawrence Axsmith
Andre Kalaser

Maury Povich
Larry Huff
Tom Campbell
Bob Kusbit
Barry Poznick
Stan Dembecki
Brian Unger
Mitchell Baum
Brad Hurtado
Rich Collier
Jim O'Connor
Barnett Adams
Kurt Hogan
Frank Horn
Ron Micca
Andrew Yinger
Dana Calderwood
Billy Kimbell
Scott Einziger
Ken Slevin
David P. Cash
Chris Darryn
Jimmy Floyd
Vinnie Potestivo
Andrew DeGiacomo
David Shenfeld
Steve Ferbber
Don McSorley
David H. Wexler
Jordan Schwartz
Bob Berkowitz
Karen Moline
Cynthia C. Muchnick
Denise Richardson
Cheryl Washington
Kathleen D. Graconia
Lippe Taylor PR
Lisa Paul
Joy Damandon
Nikki Webber
Christine Roman
Angela Ford
Elizabeth Porter
Heather Russell
Hedda Muskat
Kerri Kuliawsky
Debra Wasser
Suzanne Bersch
Marta Monahan
Kim Isaacson
Cynthia Richmond
Miranda Smith
Kathy Palmerino
Kim Swann
Angelica Holiday
Lisa Stepan
Libby Moore
Lisa Keys
Kathryn Frank-Hamlett
Kate Fergeson
Lisa McGinty
Paula Rosenthal
Jodie Roth
Felice Desner
Debbie J. Mitchell
Rita Mitchell
Shelly Palmer
John Reddman
Taha Howez
Anthony Ferror

Bill Lancaster
Annie Troche
Steven C. Schechter
Steve Sabba
Barry Goldsmith
Cecil Hollis
Randy Nkonoki-Ward
Geraldo Rivera
Jose Pretlow
Marty Bermann
Sylvia Jordan
Greg Kinnear
Sheila Jamison
Mark Wahlberg
Richard Bey
Danny Bonaduce
Jim Ryan
Larry Hoff
Bobby Rivers
Patrick Weir
Albert Aponte
Zack Van Amburg
Keith Sherman
Paul Shavelson
Frank Pioppi
Howie Mandel
Jon Purick
Ed Lover
Eric Noland
Charlie Marcus
C.J. Wambold
Joyce Simpson
Verna Moses
Lesa Walden-Young
Joni & Mark Denkins
Carolyn Wambold
Hal Hochhouser
Barbara Bevin
Robyn Patterson
Gillian Rose
Jill Spiegel
Carla Merolla
Sheri Amatenstein
Grace Cornish
Laura Lea Sanders
Sharon Jordan
Sandra Jamison
Cynthia Cowins
Deidre Sims
Angela Clowers
Vicki Burk
Zada Pachoff
Connie Kaminas
Sheila Matefy
Nicki Hedrick
Camilla Scott
Dini Petty
Andrea Webb
Kate/Rula/Joe
Leslie Seymore
Teri Kennedy
Jacquie Cannavo
Debbie Gibson
Hilery Kipnis
Amanda Weiner
Robin Feinsted
Marc J. Isaacman
Vitto Victtiro
Rakesh Mishra
Yan & Boris

Grandville
Gordon Elliot
Shannon O'Rork
Lee Fields
Rachel Frimer
Timberly Whitfield
Marilynn Fisher
Shannon Catlett
Laura Fisher
Valerie A. Worwood
Michelle Bernard
Chris Allen
Dee Dee Vincent
Phyllis Heller
Sunshine Njeri
Helen T. Shabason
Ada Cruz
Karen Glass
Marki Costello
Marian Rivman
Tracey Granstaff
Marilyn O'Reilly
Shelly Ackerman
Barbara Biziou
Laurie Sue Brockway
Judy Grafe
Dr. Judy Kuriansky
Dr. Judith Orloff
Candida Royalle
Nancy Walsh
Cheryl Cecchetto
Suzanne Jaffe
Susan Suh
Tanesha Cooper
Allison Corbliss
Jill Van Lorkan
Terry Murphy
Laura Gillis
Izzy Povich
Diane Rappaport
Robert Allen
Joe Muallem
Pam Holtz
Ann Orcut
Robyn Delin
Janice Crowder
Lissette Molina
Susan Franks
Audrey Gatling
Alexander Jewett
Raquel Ortiz
Nancy Alspaugh
Tracie Fiss
George Salongo
John Randolph Price
Juanita Dillard
Keli Lee
Kathy Bishop
Kathy Brady
Judith E. Glaser
Annie Jennings
Laura Norman
Joanne Roberts
Robin Quivers
La Teace Cuellar
Gayle Taylor
Sebastian Yeung
Satoko Shima
Haruko Konis
Shay Moore

Marilee Durgan
Mother Love
Lisa Gantz
Pucci Amanda Jones
Gigi Bell
Francis Hammond
Christina Via
Liz Anklow
Sarah Ban Breathnach
Rev. Paul Tenagia
Rev. Marianne Williamson
Rev. Richard Barnes
Rev. Eric Butterworth
Olga Butterworth
Diane Mancher & One Potata Prods.
Shadina Bell
Jose Carrion
Araceliz Cruz
Ronnie Persaud
Sean Watson
Pete Boggia
Junko Ozeki
Josui Minami
Wakca & Yika
Suruako Kataoko
Mariann Barbire
Chance Asley
Debi Ganz
Ellen Kaye
Patty Williamson
Denise Winston
Wendy Sacks
Caroline Myss Ph.D.
Rev. Catherine Ponder
4-T Prayer Group
Rev. Terry Cole-Whittaker Abraham
Shirley MacLaine
Louise L. Hay
Cecilia Bonnett
Sinbad